Curtains & Shades

Because they are made of fabric, curtains and shades introduce softness to the hard lines of a room's architecture. Fabric's folds and gathers take the edge off the right angles of windows and walls; its plush or nubbled or silken texture counterpoints wood or brick. Best of all, fabric is pliable. Anyone can shape and drape it in myriad ways to cover windows while also accomplishing a variety of decorating feats.

Together or separately, curtains and shades can frame or screen a view, control heat or sun exposure, deliver breezes or block them out. In a room with small windows, curtains mounted above and beside the frames can give the illusion of spacious glass areas. Contrariwise, curtains fitted within frames appear to bring extra-large windows down to normal size — and, in the process, expose handsome woodwork.

Corner windows can be joined by a shared treatment that emphasizes their breadth, or they may be curtained individually. Bay windows can be curtained across the wall in front of them or, to underscore their shape, inside the alcove they form: Special rods fit almost every configuration. Curtains or shades identical in style and size often will bring an impression of uniformity to mismatched windows or a mix of windows and glass doors.

Whether designed to catch the eye or blend into the background, curtains and shades become an integral part of a room's decorative scheme when they reflect the color palette and motifs that inspire the rest of the furnishings. The photographic prologue on the following pages gives a sampling of the results possible. The step-by-step instructions starting on page 18 show how easy it is to turn fabric into professional-looking curtains and shades.

Disarmingly simple in design, these unsewed curtains of flax-colored striated linen admit lavishings of sunlight by day and fade discreetly into the background at night. Stout 19th Century forged-iron nails — driven into the walls above the windows — support hand-tied knots that hold the curtains' top corners.

Cascades of raspberries and summer flowers spill prettily across the walls, cushions and windows of this rustic sitting room, giving the decorating scheme unity. The cotton window coverings, variations on roman shades, fold into place on dowels run through pockets at the back. The dowels tuck over pegs set at regular intervals along the window casing.

Rivers of red on white frame the generous-sized windows of this shore-front living room. The shades are reverse-rolled to put the roller at the back and give the fabric facing the room its trimmest finish. Hand holes centered on the rods at the bottom of the shades create pulls that are unobtrusive and sturdy.

A roman shade, constructed of tightly woven yet translucent silk, modifies the scale and importance of an ordinary apartment window — enlarging its apparent size, screening out its dull view. This neat trick is accomplished by building around the window a box frame that is high and wide, but just deep enough to hold the shade when its accordion pleats are raised and lie horizontal. Regimenting the pleats are thin plastic slats run through a channel at the bottom of every one. The rings and cords for raising and lowering the shade are concealed behind it.

A variation on the swag, this continuous drapery is the focal point of a classic wall-and-window composition. To keep the printed fabric right side out as it loops over and under the rod, the drapery maker cut the fabric into three panels and reassembled them before tacking them to the rod. The side panels are lined; the swag is both lined and interlined to give it extra body.

Breezy, voluminous curtains grace three tall windows in a Spanish country house. Made of tulle mosquito netting, their great fullness is gathered in by shirring tape stitched along the top. The tape also reinforces the headings, which are suspended from rods by curtain rings. Thus, these lighter-than-air curtains glide open and closed at the touch of a hand.

Other Publications:
THE ENCHANTED WORLD
THE KODAK LIBRARY OF CREATIVE PHOTOGRAPHY
GREAT MEALS IN MINUTES
THE CIVIL WAR
PLANET EARTH
COLLECTOR'S LIBRARY OF THE CIVIL WAR
THE EPIC OF FLIGHT
THE GOOD COOK
THE SEAFARERS
WORLD WAR II
HOME REPAIR AND IMPROVEMENT
THE OLD WEST

*For information on and a full
description of any of the Time-Life Books
series listed above, please write:*
Reader Information
Time-Life Books
541 North Fairbanks Court
Chicago, Illinois 60611

This volume is one of a series that features home decorating projects.

Curtains & Shades

by the Editors of Time-Life Books

TIME-LIFE BOOKS □ ALEXANDRIA, VIRGINIA

Time-Life Books Inc.
is a wholly owned subsidiary of
TIME INCORPORATED

FOUNDER: Henry R. Luce 1898-1967

Editor-in-Chief: Henry Anatole Grunwald
President: J. Richard Munro
Chairman of the Board: Ralph P. Davidson
Corporate Editor: Jason McManus
Group Vice President, Books: Reginald K. Brack Jr.
Vice President, Books: George Artandi

TIME-LIFE BOOKS INC.

EDITOR: George Constable
Executive Editor: George Daniels
Editorial General Manager: Neal Goff
Director of Design: Louis Klein
Editorial Board: Dale M. Brown, Roberta Conlan,
Ellen Phillips, Gerry Schremp, Gerald Simons,
Rosalind Stubenberg, Kit van Tulleken,
Henry Woodhead
Director of Research: Phyllis K. Wise
Director of Photography: John Conrad Weiser

PRESIDENT: William J. Henry
Senior Vice President: Christopher T. Linen
Vice Presidents: Stephen L. Bair, Robert A. Ellis,
John M. Fahey Jr., Juanita T. James,
James L. Mercer, Joanne A. Pello,
Paul R. Stewart, Christian Strasser

YOUR HOME

SERIES DIRECTOR: Gerry Schremp
Deputy Director: Adrian Allen
Picture Editor: Marion F. Briggs
Designer: Edward Frank (principal), Ray Ripper
Series Administrator: Loretta Y. Britten
Text Editors: Dale M. Brown, Jim Hicks,
John Newton, Peter Pocock, Lydia Preston
Staff Writers: Janet Cave Doughty,
Margery A. duMond, Allan Fallow,
Adrienne George, Kathleen M. Kiely,
Karin Kinney, Denise Li, Jane A. Martin
Copy Coordinator: Robert M. S. Somerville
Art Assistant: Jennifer B. Gilman
Picture Coordinator: Renée DeSandies
Editorial Assistant: Carolyn Wall Halbach

Special Contributors: Megan Barnett,
Sarah Brash, Anne R. Grant, Feroline Burrage
Higginson, Leslie Marshall, Wendy Buehr Murphy

Editorial Operations
Design: Ellen Robling (assistant director)
Copy Room: Diane Ullius
Editorial Operations: Caroline A. Boubin
(manager)
Production: Celia Beattie
Quality Control: James J. Cox (director),
Sally Collins
Library: Louise D. Forstall

Correspondents: Elisabeth Kraemer-Singh
(Bonn); Margot Hapgood, Dorothy Bacon
(London); Miriam Hsia (New York); Maria
Vincenza Aloisi, Josephine du Brusle (Paris);
Ann Natanson (Rome). Valuable assistance was
also provided by: Carolyn T. Chubet (New York),
Trini Bandrés (Madrid).

THE CONSULTANT

Betty Anne Ferguson has extensive background in the design and production of curtains, shades and other components of decorative and functional window coverings. She teaches in Fairfax County, Virginia, and lectures in person and on cable television.

First printing. Printed in U.S.A.

Published simultaneously in Canada.
School and library distribution by Silver Burdett Company, Morristown, New Jersey 07960.

TIME-LIFE is a trademark of
Time Incorporated U.S.A.

Library of Congress Cataloguing in
Publication Data
Main entry under title:
Curtains & shades.

(Your home)
Includes index.
1. Drapery. 2. Window-shades.
I. Time-Life Books. II. Title: Curtains and shades.
III. Series: Your home (Alexandria, Va.)
TT390.C86 1985   646.2'1   85-8425
ISBN 0-8094-5566-8
ISBN 0-8094-5567-6 (lib. bdg.)

CONTENTS

Prologue • 1

The art of dressing windows • 14
Choosing the right fabric 16
Preparing fabric for cutting 18
Matching pattern repeats 19
Basic sewing techniques 20

Classic curtains • 24
Measuring a window 25
A collection of rods 26
Understanding and installing traverse rods 28
A traverse rod on the ceiling 31
Café curtains: Simple and versatile 32
Lined curtains trimmed with bands of color 35
A scalloped treatment that stays put 40
A ruffled, double-faced style 44
The airy opulence of poufs 48
Tab curtains with threaded tiebacks 56
Bow-tied ribbons 61
A flourish of tent flaps 62
Stately swags and jabots 66
Pinch pleats in the formal tradition 72
Pleater tape 75
Pleating sheer fabrics 77
Tiebacks: The finishing touch 79
A tieback support 86
Valances: Soft skirts above the window 87
A traditional upholstered cornice 90

An array of decorative shades • 98
Leveling a shade 101
Making a fabric-covered roller shade 102
The roman style: Efficiency with flair 104
The balloon style: Lavish billows that control light 112
Sunlit patterns from dowels and layered fabric 118

Installing fasteners for window treatments • 124

Acknowledgments and picture credits 126
Index/Glossary 127

The art of dressing windows

Just as the eyes are the first things you notice in a face, so windows are natural focal points in a room. It makes good decorating sense, then, to cover and surround them with something more than routine "window dressing." The intent of this volume is to show some of the many kinds of fabric coverings that can be custom-made at home, and to spark your imagination in devising still others that are uniquely suited to your windows' needs and your decorating sensibilities.

Consider for a moment the ancient origins of window coverings. They began as plain and sturdy *ragges* hung casually over thinly glazed openings, their purpose to keep excess light and cold from pouring in. (The fact that they kept one's privacy from leaking out appears not to have mattered until quite recent times.) After dark, the cloth also made the room feel more hospitable, more intimate.

In later centuries *ragges* came to be made with greater care and were called curtains if they hung about the window frames, but shades if they were raised and lowered by some mechanism. The term "draperies" is of later coinage and, most properly, designates curtains that are long, of medium to heavy weight, and lined for opacity.

Warmth and protection remain among the basic reasons for installing curtains and shades. But the designs have become infinitely prettier and more variable, as curtains have gone from single panels to pairs, and ultimately to layered treatments combining two or more kinds of fabric plus assorted trimmings and hardware.

Perhaps no one ever used window coverings to greater effect than George Smith, whose influential designs are sampled in the 1826 hand-colored engravings opposite. Advertising himself as "Upholsterer and Furniture Draughtsman to His Majesty George IV," Smith assured readers that "drapery will ever give consequence to an apartment, and will always be adopted wherever a good taste prevails."

Consequence his creations undoubtedly gave. The designer's preferences ran to carved and gilt cornices, gold tassels and fringe, and sumptuous silks and damasks, which he deemed the natural caparisons for "persons of rank and splendid income." But Smith did not overlook persons of small fortunes either. He assured these readers that, though they might have to settle for plain valances and muslins, calicoes, and "drabs of quaker-like appear-ance, the general effect will be pleasing and in true taste" if instructions were followed carefully.

Fortunately, no one needs to settle for anything drab on the basis of budget anymore, thanks to the bountiful choice of materials available in all price ranges. As the roundup of fabrics on pages 16-17 suggests, you can find every gradation of luxury, every nuance of texture, from gossamer laces and dotted Swiss sheers to darkling damasks, in both natural fibers and easy-to-care-for synthetics. And you can select among patterns that run the gamut from tiny flower-strewn prints to bold, regimental stripes and large-scale *toiles de Jouy;* or you can have no pattern at all but a solid color chosen to provide precisely the right counterpoint for some other element in the room.

Measuring, cutting, assembling and sewing these materials depends on the simple techniques shown on pages 20-23, easily accomplished now with the aid of a sewing machine. So, too, window coverings have become easier to install as the hardware used to hang, hold back, and raise them has multiplied: Witness the devices for curtains on pages 26-31 and for shades on pages 98-101.

In the chapters following, you will learn the techniques of constructing the basic curtain *(pages 32-34):* a panel of fabric hemmed at the bottom and sides and gathered on a rod finished off by a sprightly heading. Variations and amplifications on these fundamentals yield dignified lined curtains *(pages 35-39),* as well as lightsome scalloped, ruffled and pouf styles *(pages 40-55).* For tailored applications you can choose from tab, tent-flap *(pages 56-65)* and pleated curtains *(pages 72-78).* And, with more ambition, you can fashion swags and cascades *(pages 66-71),* valances and upholstered cornices *(pages 87-97),* the likes of which can be used singly or in combinations to create a variety of formal window treatments.

Lastly, the volume will focus on fabric shades, from fit-anywhere fabric-laminated roller types *(pages 102-103)* to fancy shirred balloon styles for dressed-up windows *(pages 112-117)* and delicate gauze-and-dowel shades to complement rooms with a contemporary look *(pages 118-123).* All are appealing enough to hang on their own. And—except for the roller shades—all begin humbly enough as versions of the basic curtain. Their enrichment, as George Smith would have it, "entirely depends on the apartment they are appropriated to."

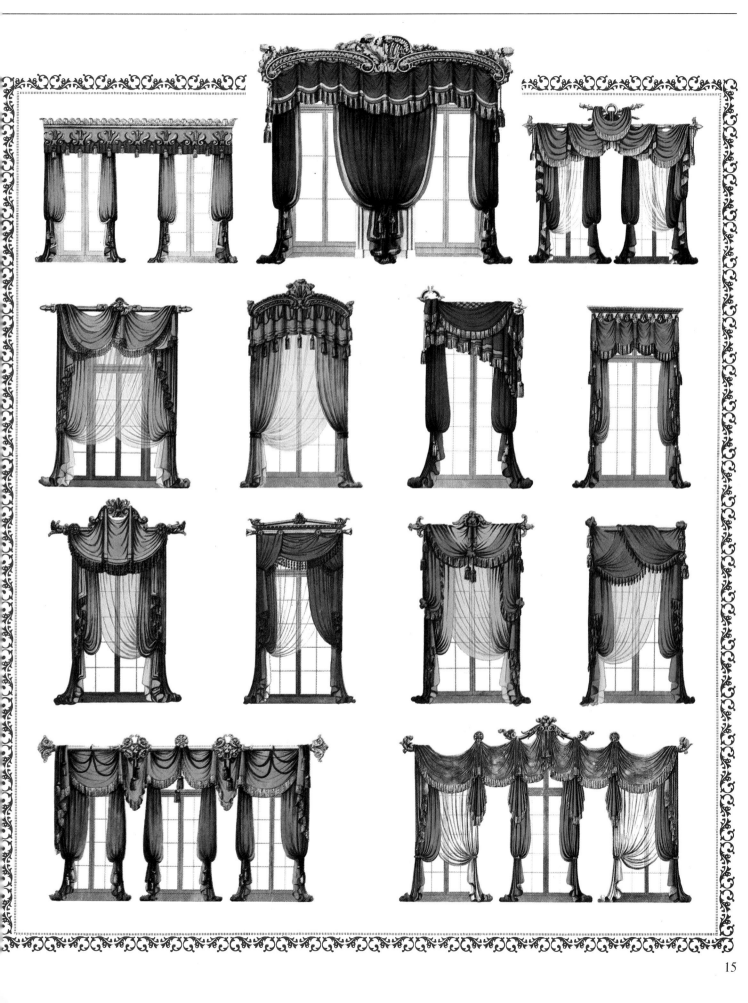

Choosing the right fabric

Out of all the elements that decorators can use to put a special stamp on their rooms, none is more exciting in its variety than fabric. For color, for texture and for pattern, the diversity of fabrics is almost endless, as the grouping below suggests.

Beyond the differences that meet the eye are those that affect wear and handling. Does the color fade after exposure to the sun? Does humidity cause the fabric to shrink or stretch? Is the fabric resistant to abrasion resulting from being drawn across the window frame?

The basic answers to these questions lie in the properties of the fibers, or threadlike strands, from which fabrics are made. As the chart at right shows, fibers are classified as either natural or man-made. Natural fibers, such as silk and cotton, excel in beauty and appealing texture. Man-made fibers, such as polyester and acrylic, are noted for easy care and resistance to moths and mildew.

Fibers may be used singly or combined in blends that bring out the desired qualities of each component. Although impossible to determine by look or feel, the fiber content of all fabrics is shown on tags attached to the bolts.

A bolt tag will also indicate whatever treatments or finishes have been given to a fabric to alter its appearance or behavior: Different treatments can make fibers resistant to creasing, abrasion, oil or water stains, fading or shrinking. Most labels suggest care for fabrics, too.

To check on how well a fabric will drape, unroll several feet from the bolt and create folds or gathers in the fabric by hand. Borrow — or, if need be, buy — a large sample you can take home to look at in the room for which it is intended; test it by day and by lamplight.

Since fabrics dyed at different times vary in hue, always begin with enough yardage to complete the job. When ordering a fabric, request a cutting of the dye lot from which yours will come.

Construction or weave is also significant. The openness of sheers and laces reveals their fragility. A tight plain weave, in which lengthwise and widthwise yarns of equal size crisscross regularly one to one, results in long-wearing fabrics such as chintz. Weaves like satin, with some yarns floating over others, are less durable; open weaves like casement, with yarns of unequal size, tend to sag.

Whatever their fabric or style, most finished curtains and shades should be frequently vacuumed; they should also be cleaned periodically by a professional dry cleaner. However, some can be laundered with warm water and soap, providing all their materials — including lining, stiffening and trim — are washable and the curtains or shades will fit in the sink or washing machine.

Fiber Characteristics at a Glance

NATURAL FIBERS	ADVANTAGES	DISADVANTAGES
Cotton	Strong, durable, versatile; withstands abrasion. Dyes easily, giving excellent color range. Takes special finishes well and can be glazed for a polished appearance.	May wrinkle or shrink if not treated. Weakened and faded by long exposure to strong sunlight. Susceptible to mildew. Soils easily unless treated. Burns unless treated.
Flax (linen)	Strong and durable. Natural untreated fiber does not support flame. Excellent color range.	Wrinkles easily and shrinks unless treated. Subject to mildew and may lose shape in damp climates. May crack along creases. Colors tend to fade in sunlight; intense colors may run in laundering. Soils easily.
Silk	Particularly strong, permitting thin but durable fabrics. Smooth, resilient and elastic. Resists mildew and wrinkles. Naturally lustrous. Drapes well. Exceptional color range.	Expensive. Weakens and fades in sunlight. Damaged by abrasion; spotted by water. Delicate in weights and constructions generally used. In humid climates, fibers are subject to mildew and rot.
Wool	Strong; resilient; not damaged by sun. Withstands abrasion in tightly woven fabrics. Slow to wrinkle or soil. Resists flame. Drapes well. Excellent color range. Will hold color depth over a long period.	Shrinks unless treated. Susceptible to moths and mildew. Usually not washable. Tends to accumulate static electricity.

MAN-MADE FIBERS	ADVANTAGES	DISADVANTAGES
Acetate	Resists mildew and moths. Economical. Drapes well. Dyes easily, giving a good color range. Looks like silk when blended with other fibers. Gives fabrics luxurious feel and appearance.	Injured by abrasion; weakened by sunlight. Melts at low heat. Fades unless labeled "solution-dyed." Usually not washable. Accumulates static electricity unless treated.
Acrylic	Withstands abrasion, mildew, moths, fading and wrinkling. Not damaged by sunlight. Slow to soil; easy to spot-clean. Holds color well.	Accumulates static electricity unless treated.
Glass	Flameproof. Colorfast. Resistant to damage by sun, moths and mildew. Will not shrink or wrinkle. Slow to soil; easy to spot-clean. Drapes well; lustrous, silky. Can be woven into very sheer fabrics.	Poor abrasion tolerance. May crack along folds if creased; may splinter and scratch when handled. Limited color range. Needs to be hand-washed: Wear gloves to avoid cuts from the brittle fibers.
Modacrylic	Resists wrinkles, damage from sun, mildew and moths. Flameproof. Holds creases well; slow to soil. Colorfast. Good color range.	Poor abrasion tolerance; not very strong. Melts at low heat. Accumulates static electricity unless treated.
Nylon	Strongest fiber. Durable, withstands abrasion; resists moths, mildew and wrinkling. Recovers shape if stretched. Slow to soil; easy to spot-clean. Dries rapidly. Good color range.	Accumulates static electricity unless treated. Fades and tends to weaken in sunlight.
Polyester	Strong and durable. Withstands abrasion. Resists moths, mildew and wrinkles. Drapes well. Holds shape well and stays crisp. Dyes moderately well, giving reasonably good color range.	Accumulates static electricity unless treated. Susceptible to oil stains.
Rayon	Versatile; relatively strong. Economical. Highly absorbent. Dyes well and has excellent color range. Drapes well. Looks like silk when combined with other fibers.	Lacks resilience. Injured by abrasion; damaged by sun; susceptible to mildew. Wrinkles easily. Cannot be laundered. Poor resistance to fire.

Preparing fabric for cutting

Nothing makes a curtain or shade look more professional than straight seams, neat edges and precisely matched fabric designs. The first step in achieving this goal is to square the fabric's cut edges. The threads in woven fabrics are set at right angles to one another on the loom, so an unpatterned fabric or a fabric with a woven pattern is intrinsically squared. However, it may be pulled out of shape when lengths are cut from the bolt at the fabric store. You can rectify this problem simply by pulling out a thread spanning the fabric's width and cutting along the line left behind (below).

Printed patterns seldom follow the direction of the threads, and pulling a thread will not serve to straighten the design. Squaring a print requires drawing across the fabric a line that is perpendicular to the design, not the selvages, then cutting on the line. Depending on the width of the fabric, you will need a yardstick, a 48-inch ruler or a combination of rulers fastened end to end with tape for marking the line.

Furthermore, some fabrics — patterned or not — are treated with finishes that makes pulling out a thread impossible. Chintz is one such fabric; you will find others by trial and error. For these, use a carpenter's square or a T square to draw a chalk line perpendicular to the selvage, and cut along that line.

When working with any patterned fabric, measure out enough material so that you can match repeated details in its design; each panel must be not only equal in length, but also identical in design. This way the designs along the selvage of one panel will match the designs along the selvage of another panel (opposite, bottom).

To calculate the total amount of fabric you need for an unpatterned curtain or shade, simply multiply the unfinished length by the number of panels needed to cover the width of your window. To determine how much of a printed fabric you need, first measure one pattern repeat — the lengthwise distance from the center of one detail within the fabric's design to the center of the next identical detail. Then divide the curtain's unfinished length by the length of one pattern repeat; round the figure up to the next whole number. Multiply this number by the length of the pattern repeat. The resulting figure is the length each panel should be cut. For example, if a pattern repeat is 12 inches and the unfinished length of your curtain is 70 inches, each panel should be cut to 72 inches (six pattern repeats). The 2 inches of excess is trimmed only after the panels are sewed together. Finally, multiply the number of panels needed to cover the width of your window by the panel length. The answer is the total amount of fabric you need to buy.

Squaring Plain Fabric and Woven Patterns

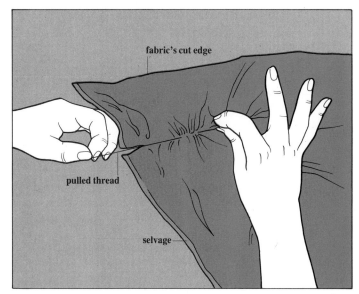

fabric's cut edge

pulled thread

selvage

1 **Pulling a thread from the selvage.** Spread out the fabric on a large, flat work surface. Use scissors to snip the tight weave of the selvage nearest you, cutting at a point about 3 inches from the fabric's end. Pick out a loose thread and pull it gently. As you pull, gradually slide small sections of the fabric backward along the thread (above).

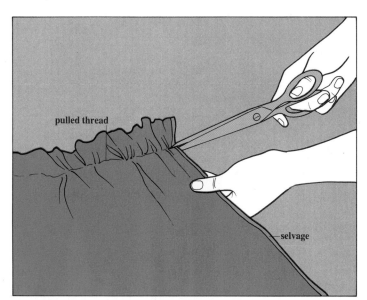

pulled thread

selvage

2 **Cutting the selvage to release the thread.** When the fabric's entire width is puckered and you reach the opposite selvage, make another cut in the selvage to release the thread (above). Pull out the thread and smooth the fabric. Cut the fabric along the line left by the pulled thread.

Squaring Fabric with a Printed Pattern

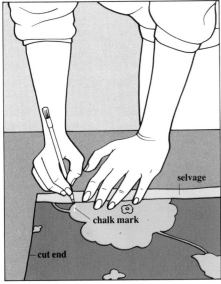

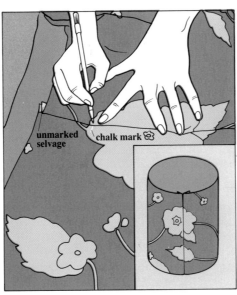

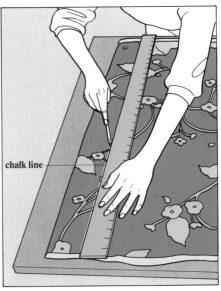

1 **Marking the pattern.** Spread the fabric flat, right side up, on a large table. Roughly 3 inches from the cut end, make a chalk mark on the patterned part of the fabric next to the selvage nearest you.

2 **Matching the design.** Turn the fabric over and bring the edges of the two selvages together. Fold under the unmarked selvage and place it over the marked selvage. Carefully match the design *(inset)*. Then extend the chalk mark onto the folded edge of the fabric *(above)*.

3 **Marking the cutting line.** Unfold the fabric and turn it right side up again. Align each end of a long ruler with the chalk marks. Holding the ruler firmly in place, connect the two marks with a straight chalk line. Cut along this line with scissors.

Matching Pattern Repeats

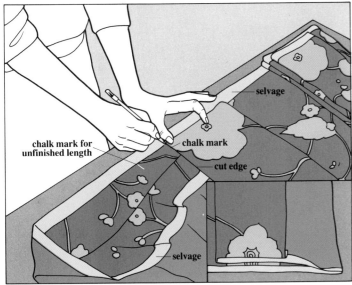

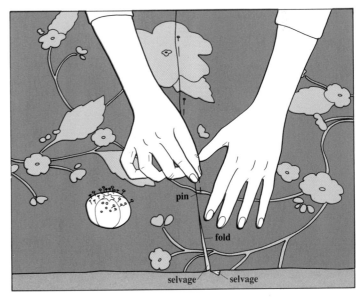

1 **Finding the repeat.** Unroll the fabric and mark the unfinished length along one selvage. Unroll more fabric until you see the repeat of the cut edge's design. Bring the printed side of the fabric's cut edge to the repeat. Fold under the selvage and match the patterns *(inset)*. Then mark the bottom layer where the cut edge rests *(above)*. Repeat this step along the other selvage. Connect the marks with a line and cut along it. Use this first width as a template to cut as many widths as you need.

2 **Pinning panels together.** Lay two panels lengthwise on the work surface so that their selvages are side by side. Fold under the selvage of one panel and place it on top of the selvage of the other panel. Adjust the panels until their patterns fit together. Then, pin them together by inserting pins at regular intervals through both selvages.

Basic sewing techniques

Even fancy curtains and shades are made with straight seams and basic stitches that require only elementary sewing skills. A sewing machine speeds the work, but it is not essential. In fact, some seams, such as side hems, are best completed by hand.

Whether you sew by machine or by hand, there are three types of stitches to master: straight, overcast (also called zigzag) and blind-hem (*pages 21-23*). Straight stitches are used to join lengths of fabric, form rod casings or pleats, and do topstitching — a visible line sewed on the fabric face. Overcast stitches keep raw edges from unraveling. And blind-hem stitches attach a hem to the back of fabric so the stitches are barely visible on the fabric face.

When setting up a machine for sewing, first thread it as directed in the owner's manual, winding the bobbin if necessary. Once the upper and lower threads are in place, adjust the tensions (*opposite, upper right*). Both threads should be drawn equally tight so they will lock in the center of each stitch; otherwise, the seam will pucker. The thread tensioner on the machine adjusts the upper thread, and a bobbin screw regulates the lower thread.

Choice of thread also affects a seam's smoothness. Generally, you should use synthetic thread with synthetic fabrics and natural thread with natural fabrics so fabric and thread will shrink at the same rate during cleaning. However, many fabrics have finishes that can cause them to react uncharacteristically: Cotton, for example, may be preshrunk. Before starting to sew, wash a fabric scrap that has been sewed with the thread to test their compatibility. Or choose so-called dual-duty thread, a cotton-covered polyester that works well with almost all fabrics.

Thread and needle thicknesses are also important. Dual-duty thread is equivalent in size to the old standard No. 50 and is suitable for most curtain and shade fabrics; extra-fine thread suits sheers; and heavyweight thread is used for topstitching. Size 9 and 11 needles suit lightweight fabrics, a size 14 suits medium-weight fabrics and a size 16 heavy fabrics.

Stitch length, too, affects the seam. Short stitches may cause a seam to pucker, especially when they hold a number of layers of fabric. For that reason, fairly long stitches — eight to the inch — are recommended for most projects in this book.

Seams should be sewed about ½ inch from the edge of the fabric. For a seam along the tightly woven fabric edge called the selvage, use scissors to make small cuts in the selvage perpendicular to the seam line every 3 to 4 inches. This keeps the selvage, which is woven tighter than the rest of the fabric, from shrinking more than the fabric. If the selvage is wider than ½ inch and has a printed edge, sew the seam ½ inch inside the selvage, then cut off the selvage and overcast the raw edges by machine or by hand (*page 22*).

The machine and its parts. Although models differ, every sewing machine uses two threads: an upper thread guided from the spool to the needle and a lower thread brought up from the bobbin. The bobbin (*inset*) is an encased spindle around which the lower thread is wound. There are different dials to select the type of stitch and the length and width of the stitch. A clamp called the presser foot holds the fabric in place beneath the needle. The fabric is pulled forward by a toothed plate, called the feed dog, which is beneath the presser foot. To start the first stitch, turn the handwheel located on the side of the machine.

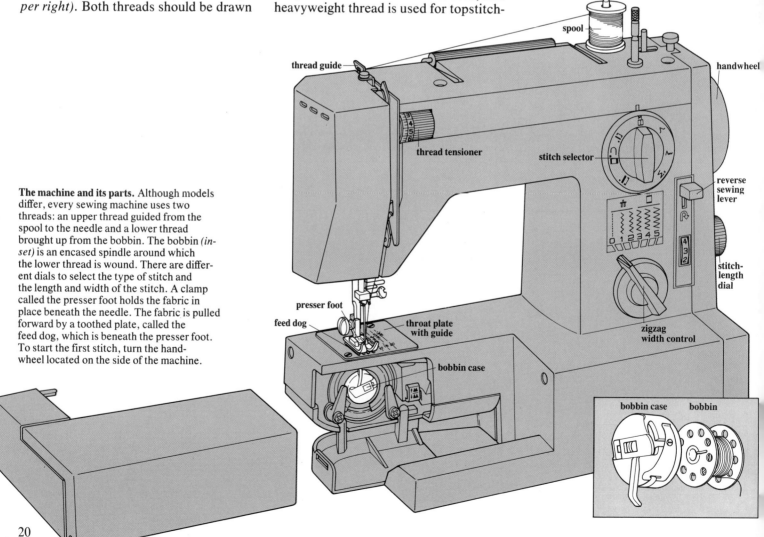

spool

thread guide

handwheel

thread tensioner

stitch selector

reverse sewing lever

stitch-length dial

presser foot

feed dog

throat plate with guide

zigzag width control

bobbin case

bobbin case   bobbin

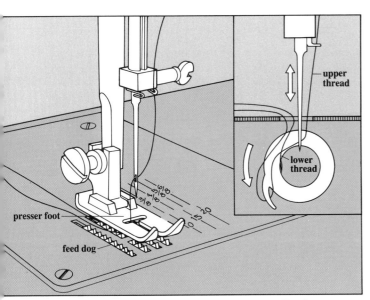

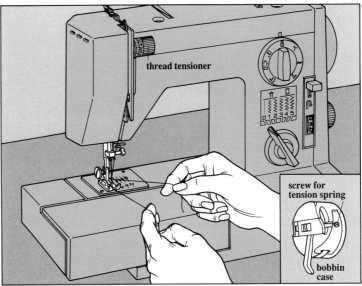

Pulling up the bobbin thread. Wind the bobbin, thread the needle of the machine with the upper thread, then insert the bobbin — all according to the owner's manual. Grasp the end of the upper thread and turn the handwheel toward you; the upper thread will tighten around the lower thread wrapped on the bobbin *(inset),* pulling it up in a loop. Pull the end of the lower thread from the loop and draw out both threads 3 or 4 inches. Bring the ends together to the rear of the presser foot.

Adjusting the tension. Pull both the upper and lower threads toward you. They should be equally taut. If the upper thread feels too tight, turn the thread tensioner down one or two points; if the tension feels too loose, turn the dial up one or two points. To adjust the tension on the lower thread, tighten or loosen the tension spring by turning a screw in the bobbin case *(inset).* Pull the threads toward the back and try out a few stitches on a scrap of the fabric that you plan to use. When the tension is equal, you are ready to begin your project.

Sewing a straight machine seam. Fasten the layers of the fabric with straight pins placed 2 inches apart at right angles to the intended seam line: In this case, the seam joins two layers of fabric placed with their right, or finished, sides together. Use the handwheel to raise the needle, and slide the pinned fabric edge under it; align the edge with the 4/8-inch guide on the throat plate to leave a seam allowance of ½ inch *(inset).*

Lower the needle into the fabric and then lower the presser foot. Turn the stitch-length dial to 0. Lock the first stitch of the seam by sewing three or four stitches in place. Turn the stitch-length dial to eight stitches to the inch and begin sewing, guiding the fabric with your hands as the feed dog pulls it forward. At the end of the seam, turn the stitch-length dial back to 0 and lock-stitch again. Raise the presser foot and the needle, pull out the fabric and cut the threads, leaving tag ends 6 inches long.

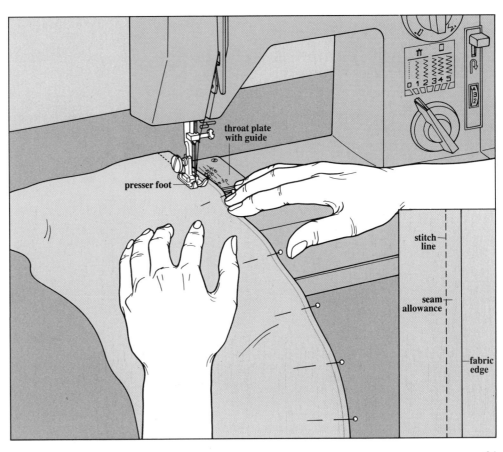

21

Forestalling Raveling on Raw Seams

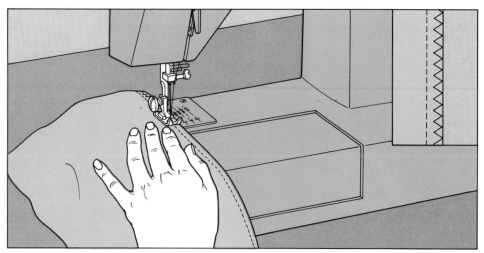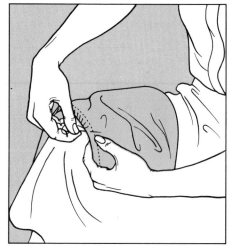

Overcasting by machine. Turn the stitch selector to the zigzag stitch. Place the needle on the edge of the fabric, set the stitch-length dial at 0 and lower the presser foot. Turn the handwheel to start the first stitch. Sew three stitches in place to lock your seam. Then set the stitch-length dial at eight stitches to the inch and turn the zigzag width control to ¼ inch. Sew along the fabric, overcasting the raw edge *(inset)*. At the end of the seam, sew three lock stitches.

Overcasting by hand. Thread a needle and knot the two ends together to make a double thread. Anchor the knot on the inside of the seam; pull the needle through the fabric. With the thread to the right, insert the needle under the fabric ⅛ to ¼ inch to the left of the first stitch. Stitch to the end of the seam, then insert the needle ¼ inch behind the last stitch, bringing it out where the last stitch ended to secure the thread firmly.

Blind-hem Stitching by Hand

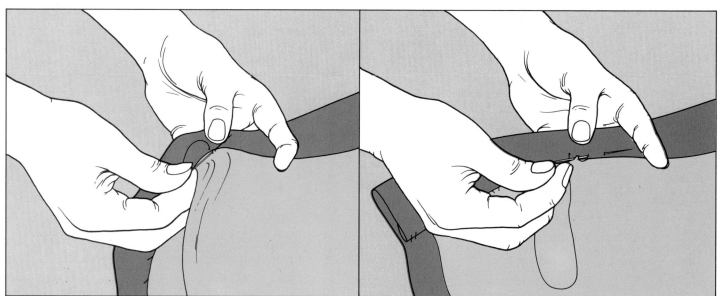

Blind-hem stitching by hand. Use a single thread with a knot in the end. Working from right to left, hide the knot on the inside of the hem and draw the needle through the hem fabric. With the needle, pick up one or two of the fabric threads from the wrong, or unfinished, side of the face of the fabric close to the hem edge *(above)*. Then slide the needle hori-zontally through the folded edge of the hem for about ½ inch *(above)* and pull the thread through. Make evenly spaced stitches along the hem fold, and end with the fastening stitch used in overcasting by hand.

Blind-hem Stitching by Machine

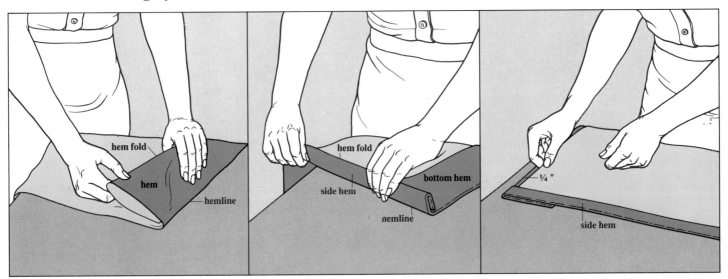

1 **Folding the curtain fabric.** From the wrong, or unfinished, side of the bottom of the curtain, fold the fabric over on itself and then over again to create a double fold for the bottom hem *(above, left)*. Press the folds in place. Turn over a double side hem *(above, center)* and press it flat. Fold the opposite side hem; press it. Pin the hems in place. Now fold the bottom hem under so that only ¼ inch of the inside top edge of the hem shows *(above, right)*.

2 **Sewing the hem.** Lower the needle into the edge of the hem, lower the presser foot and lock-stitch for three or four stitches. Reset the machine on blind-hem stitch at a length of eight stitches to the inch and a width of ¼ inch. Then sew along the edge, lining the edge up against the throat-plate guide so you will sew four straight stitches on the hem and one zigzag stitch across to the front *(inset)*. The zigzag stitch will catch only one or two threads in the fabric's face and hence be nearly invisible from the front. Keep sewing in this manner to the end of the hem, then lock-stitch again.

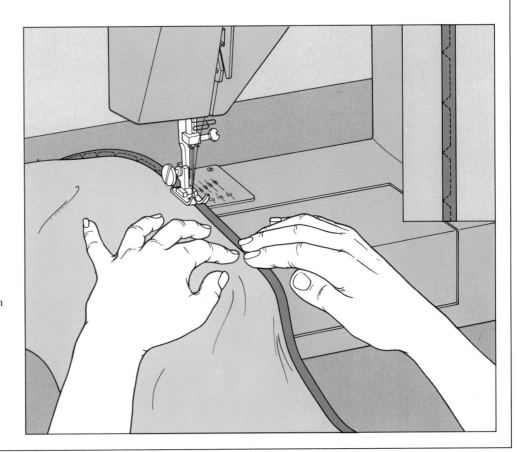

Classic curtains

Curtains all begin as simple fabric panels. The seemingly limitless variety of styles arising from such humble origins is a result of the different ways fabric can be cut, gathered—and hung. In fact, the rod from which a pair of curtains hangs is integral to its shape.

Curtains are divided into two categories: stationary and movable. Stationary curtains, fixed to rods or boards in artful folds, are mainly decorative. The burden of light and privacy control falls on shades, blinds or a layer of movable curtains. Stationary curtains can hang from a rod run through a casing in the top of the fabric or from hooks attached to a flat metal rod (pages 26-27). Tent-flap styles, swags and jabots generally are tacked to wood mounting boards (pages 63 and 67).

Movable curtains, which slide back and forth, can hang from rings on the rods used for stationary curtains. But curtains that are often opened and closed usually hang on cord-and-pulley-operated traverse rods (pages 28-31).

Other than the swinging crane rod (page 27), which must be specially ordered, all of the rods shown in this book can be found at department stores, fabric shops or hardware stores. Rods are commonly stocked in lengths from 30 inches to 12 feet, and most adjust to fit the width of any standard window.

After determining which kind of rod you need for the curtain you are making, follow the guidelines opposite to measure your window. (A double-hung sash window is illustrated, but the principles it demonstrates apply to other styles.) Use these measurements to determine the size of the rod and the location of its mounting brackets. Install the rod before figuring out your fabric requirements.

Most curtain rods are outside-mounted—attached to the window frame, the wall or the ceiling. However, rods for café curtains and curtains hung as undertreatments are frequently inside-mounted—attached to the jambs inside the window recess. A few rods, such as those on French doors or inward-opening casement windows, are sash-mounted—attached to the movable part of the window.

To present a neat appearance from outside the house, curtains suspended from rings or hooks are hung at least 5 inches above the glass, thus concealing the hardware from view. Extend rods for movable curtains far enough past the window to hold the drawn curtain fabric, called "stackback," clear of the glass when the curtain is open.

Unlike shades, which must be level in order to function properly (page 101), curtain rods generally are not leveled. Because most houses do not have perfectly level ceilings, or perfectly square window frames, a level rod can look disconcertingly crooked. A rod mounted above the frame should parallel the ceiling line; one installed below the top of the frame should parallel the frame's upper edge.

Most rods are sold with end brackets and mounting screws. If the rod is longer than 4 feet, use intermediate support brackets as well. Screws, however, are not adequate fasteners unless the rod will be mounted on the window frame or on a nonmasonry wall within inches of the frame, in which case the screws will pierce wood structural members that support the window. In other situations check the appendix (pages 124-125) for appropriate alternative fasteners.

The distance from the rod to the mounting surface is known as the rod return. If the rod brackets are mounted on the wall, the return should be wide enough so that the rod clears the window frame and sill.

After installing the rod, you can take its measure for calculating to the inch how much fabric you should buy. To ensure accuracy, use a steel tape or folding wood ruler.

First measure the rod from corner to corner and multiply by three or by the width allowance specified for the style of curtains you are making. Add twice the rod return. (For example, if the rod projects 3 inches from the wall, add 6 inches). If the curtains will overlap, add 4 more inches. Divide the total by the width of the fabric you have chosen and round off the result to the nearest whole number. This final figure is the number of widths of fabric you need.

Next, calculate length by measuring from the top of the rod to where you want the bottom of the curtain. Add the inches needed for top and bottom hems. (Hem depths for projects in this book are given with the instructions.) The result is the so-called cut, or unfinished, length. If the fabric is patterned, divide the cut length by the inches in a repeat; round off the result to the next-highest figure to find the number of repeats for each length. Multiply this figure by the inches in a repeat to adjust the cut length.

Finally, multiply the cut length (or adjusted cut length) by the number of widths. Divide this final figure by 36 to find the number of yards of fabric you must buy.

Measuring a Window

Calculating width.

● For inside-mounted rods, measure from side jamb to side jamb wherever you want the curtain top (**AA**). For curtains mounted across the lower sash, measure the window width at a point high enough above the meeting rail to clear the lock. To make sure the window recess is deep enough to accommodate any inside-mounted rod, plus gathered curtain fabric, measure from the face of the inner sash to the front edge of the frame.

● For outside-mounted rods or mounting boards attached to the window frame, measure across the frame from outer edge to outer edge (**BB**). If the rod or board is to be mounted on the wall, add the distance it will extend beyond the frame.

● For movable curtains on outside-mounted rods, add enough extra room beyond the glass area for stackback (**CC**): Allow at least one third the width of the window opening (or of the glass you want to expose when the curtains are open). If your fabric is bulky, add an additional inch for every width of fabric you will use. For curtains that will part in the center, divide the stackback equally on each side of the window; for one-way draw curtains, extend the rod the entire stackback length to one side.

Calculating length.

● For curtains hung on inside-mounted rods or rods mounted on the window frame, measure from the top of the rod to the window sill (**DD** and **EE**).

● For curtains hung on wall-mounted rods, to conceal the hardware from outside view, measure up 5 inches or more from the top of the window opening (**FF**). Then, using a metal tape measure or a folding wood ruler, measure from the ceiling line down to that point. Mark that distance at several more points across the wall to establish exactly where the top of the rod will go.

● For sill-length curtains that are hung on wall-mounted rods, measure from the top of the rod to the sill and subtract ¼ inch for clearance (**GG**).

● For apron-length curtains hung on wall-mounted rods — that is, curtains long enough to cover the broad wood strip or skirt below the window sill — measure from the top of the rod to the bottom of the apron and add at least 1 inch (**HH**).

● For floor-length curtains hung on wall-mounted rods, measure from the top of the rod to the floor and subtract ½ inch for clearance (**II**). Double-check floor-length measurements by measuring at several points along the rod. If your floor is uneven, subtract the ½ inch from the shortest measurement to allow for adequate clearance.

A collection of rods

Inside-mounted rod. The café curtains on pages 32-34, like most inside-mounted curtains, are hung on tension rods — telescoping steel tubes with an interior spring. The spring pushes the rubber- or plastic-tipped ends of the tube outward against the window jambs to hold the rod in place.

Curtains hung from inside-mounted rods are generally sill length, hanging from the top of the rod to the sill, minus ¼ inch for clearance. If your curtains will hang from rings, subtract the distance from the top of the rod to the bottom of the ring *(left inset)* to determine the curtains' finished length. If they will have a heading above the rod, add the height of the additional fabric *(right inset)* to get the finished length.

Sash rods. The curtain on pages 40-43 is stretched between a pair of sash rods, mounted parallel on shallow brackets placed above and below the glass area of a door. The same treatment could be used for an inward-opening casement window or for any window — in a kitchen, perhaps, or a bathroom — where the fabric must be kept under tight control. The brackets above the window are mounted with their U-shaped slots facing up; the ends of the rod rest in the brackets. Below the window, the brackets are reversed *(inset);* the rod, run through rings or a hem at the bottom of the curtain, is held in place by the taut fabric.

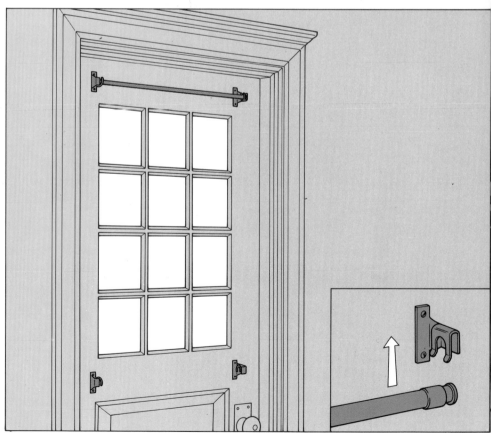

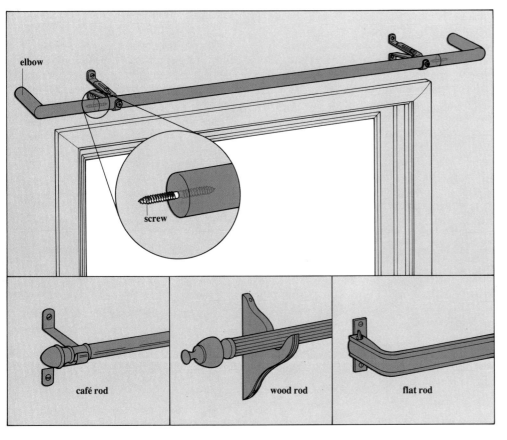

Outside-mounted rod. The casing-top curtains on pages 35-39 and pages 48-55 hang on wood rods fitted with elbows that are pushed through the casing so that the curtain's outer edge touches the wall and turns an uninterrupted corner. The wood elbows (attached by concealed screws) can be sawed to create the desired rod return. The rods are supported by metal brackets that adjust to provide between 2½ and 3½ inches of rod return. The fabric casing is slit at the back to accommodate the bracket ends.

Similar brackets support the café rods *(left inset)* used for lightweight outside-mounted café curtains. The tab curtains on pages 56-60 are hung from rods supported by decorative wood brackets and tipped with ornamental finials *(center inset)*. Tab or casing-top curtains may also be suspended from flat metal rods mounted on simple hooked brackets *(right inset)*.

To determine the rod returns for these styles, measure straight out from the wall to the front edge of the rod. Most curtains hung on outside-mounted rods are apron length or floor length; as illustrated opposite, adjust the measurements to account for rings or headings.

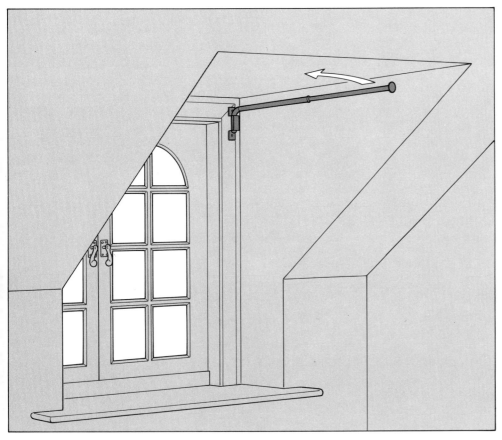

Swinging drapery crane. The ruffled curtain on pages 44-47 is gathered on a drapery crane, a brass rod projecting from a bracket screwed to the window frame. The crane, which is adjustable up to 2 feet in length, pivots in the bracket, allowing the curtain to be swung over the window for privacy. The crane comes with optional curtain rings and is available in enameled metal as well as brass. The bracket shown and its mate (concealed by the window recess) are screwed into the window frame at its top outside corners.

Understanding and installing traverse rods

Though complex compared with other rods, a traverse rod is still quite simple: In essence, it is nothing more than a flat metal tube with an open channel at the back, as this rear view shows. The channel contains movable slides with holes for the curtain hooks. Traverse rods come as two-way draws, opening in the center, or one-way draws, pulling a single curtain to either the right or left.

The traverse rod comes fully assembled, fitted with the cord that makes the curtains traverse. In the two-way draw version below, the long section of cord *(light gray)* is tied to the rod's principal moving part, the overlap master slide,

and is threaded through the tube *(light gray arrows)* and over a pulley wheel at the end of the rod. The cord is doubled back through the rod. A second master slide, the underlap slide, is hooked to the doubled-back section of cord. The cord continues through the rod, past the overlap slide and over another pulley wheel. A tug on the cord pulls the master slides toward each other, closing the curtain.

The shorter section of the cord *(dark gray)* is also attached to the overlap slide; it runs in the opposite direction *(dark gray arrows)*, over another pulley wheel at the end of the rod. A tug on this cord pulls the overlap slide toward one end and reverses the direction of the other cord,

pulling the underlap slide to the opposite end: The curtains are thus drawn open.

The cord forms a long loop that is held taut by a cord tension pulley mounted at the floor or window frame. The loop usually hangs from the right side of the rod, but you can reverse its position. To do this, grasp the cord that loops over the pulley wheel at the other side of the rod and pull it all the way through the rod.

A curtain is hooked to both the master and the carrier slides. The number of carrier slides is determined by the number of pleats in the curtain *(page 73)*. To remove surplus carrier slides, push up the end gates attached to the pulley housings and slip the extras out of the channel.

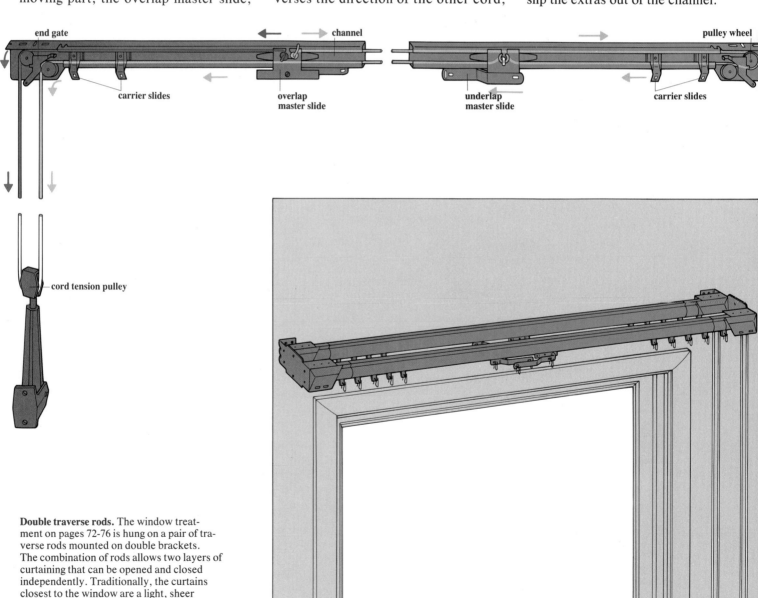

Double traverse rods. The window treatment on pages 72-76 is hung on a pair of traverse rods mounted on double brackets. The combination of rods allows two layers of curtaining that can be opened and closed independently. Traditionally, the curtains closest to the window are a light, sheer fabric while the outer curtains, or draperies, are of heavier, opaque material.

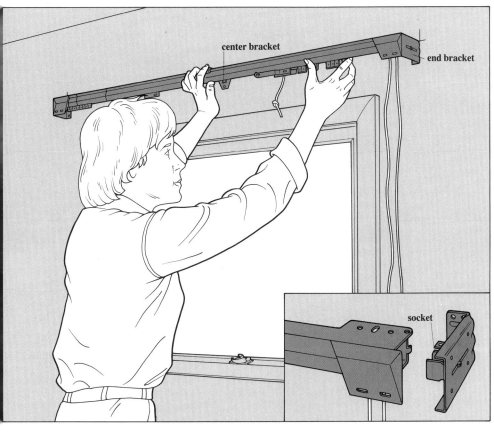

center bracket

end bracket

socket

1 **Mounting end brackets.** Following the measuring guidelines on page 25, mark the height of the rod and its position on each side of the window. Hold the top edge of an end bracket, its U-shaped socket facing upward *(inset),* at the height marks on one side, and mark the position of each screw hole. Repeat for the opposite end bracket.

Drill screw holes at each mark, then attach the brackets to the wall, using the screws supplied by the manufacturer or one of the fasteners illustrated on page 125.

Hook the lipped support clip of the center bracket over the rod at its midpoint, then lift the rod into position, fitting its ends into the mounted end brackets *(left).*

support clip

bracket

cam

2 **Attaching the center bracket.** Mark the screw holes for the center bracket *(left),* take the rod down, and remove the center bracket and its support clip. Drill holes for the bracket, then mount it. Lift the rod into position once more, snapping the center support clip over the top of the rod and hooking the clip into the groove at the front.

To lock the support clip in place, use a screwdriver to turn the metal cam on the underside of the clip *(seen from behind in inset)* counterclockwise until it snaps firmly into the groove at the back of the rod. ▶

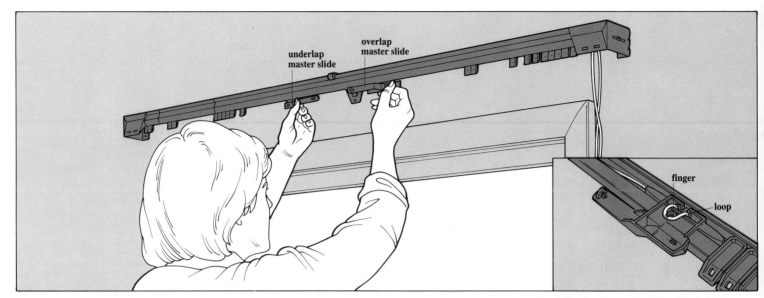

underlap
master slide

overlap
master slide

finger

loop

3 **Adjusting the master slides.** Push the overlap and underlap master slides to opposite ends of the rod. At the left-hand end, reach behind the underlap slide for the cord; you will feel it running just above the small plastic finger that projects from the back of the slide *(inset, above)*. Pull the cord out about an inch to form a small loop and carefully hook it over the finger, making sure the loop is securely anchored.

excess cord

6 **Adjusting cord length.** Reach behind the overlap master slide to locate the two knots at its back *(inset, left)*. Grasp the knot nearest the carrier slides, and pull downward until the cord hanging at the side of the rod is pulled taut against the pulley wheel. Tie a new knot in the cord at the back of the overlap slide, allowing the excess cord to hang slack below. Remove the nail in the inner stem of the pulley, then cut off the extra cord and tighten the knot securely.

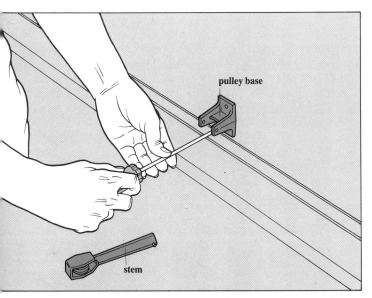

pulley base

stem

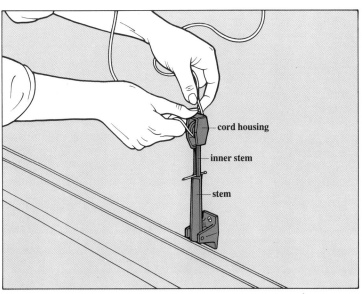

cord housing

inner stem

stem

4 **Mounting the pulley base.** Detach the stem of the pulley from the pulley base, then hold the base against the wall close to the floor, directly below a point 2 inches in from the right-hand end of the rod. (In this position it will be concealed by the hanging curtain.) Mark the position of each mounting hole on the wall, then drill screw holes at the marks. Attach the pulley base with screws or other suitable fasteners, depending on the composition of the wall.

5 **Attaching the cord to the pulley.** Reattach the stem of the pulley to the base. Pull up on the cord housing to expose the hole on the inner stem. Insert a small nail through the hole to keep the stem fully extended. Then slip the looped end of the cord through the slot in the cord housing.

A Traverse Rod on the Ceiling

With only minor modifications, the type of traverse rod that is mounted on a wall can be mounted on the ceiling. The rod is attached to the ceiling by fasteners pushed through holes in the pulley housing at each end of the rod. If the rod needs center support, the center support clip may be attached directly to the ceiling. The center bracket and the end brackets customarily used to mount the rods on a wall are not needed.

To mount a rod on the ceiling, first detach the center support mounting bracket from the center support clip by removing the attaching screw and nut. Then snap the clip onto the rod, as in Step 1, page 29. Next, hold the rod against the ceiling and use a pencil to mark the position of the screw holes in the pulley housings and the center support clip. Take the rod down, then drill holes at all of the marks. Hold the rod against the ceiling once again and fasten it with wood screws or other appropriate fasteners (*pages 124-125*).

An alternative to conventional traverse rods is the ceiling track, a metal channel containing plastic slides. It lacks cords and pulleys, making it less bulky and conspicuous than a traverse rod. However, the curtain that hangs from it must be opened and closed manually. The track can be ordered cut to length through a drapery retailer. It is mounted on the ceiling through holes spaced at intervals along the channel.

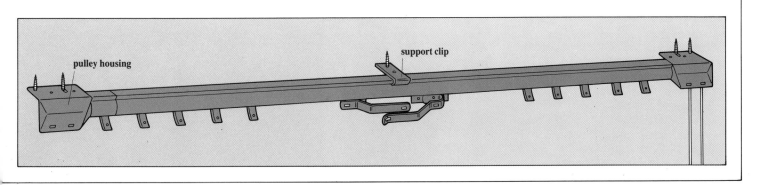

pulley housing

support clip

Café curtains: Simple and versatile

Café curtains, which allow you to see out without letting the world see in, are among the most popular of window treatments. One reason is their versatility. They can be hung in pairs covering half windows, as here, or in overlapping tiers that can be opened and closed independently. Like these, they can be made with casings at the top to slip over rods, or they can hang from rings sewed to a scalloped top edge *(pages 40-43)* or from tabs of fabric *(pages 58-59)*.

The fabric, too, can vary to suit almost any décor. Lace bestows formality on an otherwise informal curtain; sheer and semisheer materials serve as lightweight filters to screen the outside world; and plain or patterned opaque fabrics can echo or accent colors and designs used elsewhere in a room.

Besides being versatile, café curtains are very easy to make. While they can be embellished with features like scalloped or tabbed edges, in their basic form they are the simplest, most fundamental of curtain panels — and as such can serve as a valuable primer for a novice curtain maker. (The ones pictured here are just one step away from the simplest form; these have a heading — a decorative margin of fabric that stands above the rod — which requires only one more seam than a casing without a heading.)

To estimate how much material you need, see the general information about measuring on pages 24-25, as well as Step 1, opposite, which tells how to calculate the fabric required for one of these curtains. The width of fabric recommended here — triple the width the curtain is to cover — is for lace or sheer material. A double width will do for heavyweight fabrics that cannot be gathered tightly on the rod or for patterns better displayed without deep folds. If dealing with a pattern, remember, also, to take the size of the repeat into account when making your calculations *(pages 18-19)*.

Because lace and sheer fabrics are sold in widths as great as 118 inches, it is rarely necessary to sew widths together to create a sufficiently wide panel. If you are using a wide lace of exceptionally fine quality, consider making a single panel, rather than two, to cover the whole width of the window, thereby avoiding cutting and sewing that might injure the lace.

These curtains hang from tension rods *(page 26)* mounted inside the window frame. These thin rods make no appreciable difference to the length of fabric required for a curtain, but the circumference of a thick rod should be taken into consideration *(page 36, Step 1)*. Because this is an inside mount, the curtains reach to the window sill. If mounted outside, they could hang lower to cover the window's apron, the board below the sill.

The secret of curtains that hang well is in the weights sewed into their bottom edges *(Step 4)* and in the smoothness of their hems. All curtain hems are doubled to keep raw edges hidden. They must be folded to exact measurements and pressed in place before being sewed. Hems in most fabrics should be pressed with a steam iron, but some delicate materials, such as antique satin, should instead be ironed dry, because steam can leave water marks. And steam can shrink the selvages of some other cloths. Always test a scrap to be sure the fabric you are using can be steam-ironed.

Depending on the material's weight, use a fine No. 9 or No. 11 needle to sew lace, sheer or semisheer fabric.

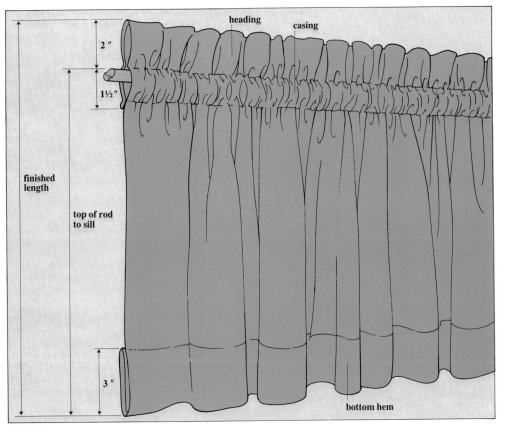

heading casing

2"

1½"

finished length

top of rod to sill

3"

bottom hem

1 **Calculating fabric dimensions.** Measure from the top of the rod to the window sill, subtracting ¼ inch for clearance, and add the height of the heading. The result is the curtain's finished length. To determine the total length of fabric required for a curtain like the one shown in this cutaway drawing, first add to the finished length the amount needed for a bottom hem — here, 6 inches for a 3-inch double hem. Next, add the amount needed to form a double-thick backing for the rod casing; this casing is 1½ inches high, so allow 3 inches. Finally, add double the height of the heading — here, 4 inches for the 2-inch heading.

To find the width of a curtain panel when two panels are to hang at a window, multiply half the rod's length by three, so the curtain's width will be triple that of the space it covers. The fabric need only approximate this width; one selvage-to-selvage fabric width will probably serve for each panel. (See page 36, Step 2, for instructions on making up wider panels.)

Following the horizontal line of the lace design, cut as many panels as you need. When cutting, match each section to the first one by aligning the lace pattern along the selvage (*page 19*).

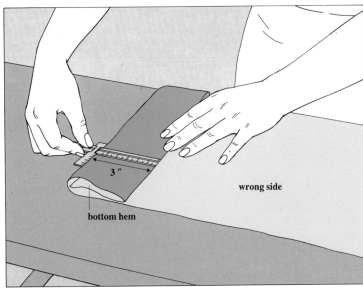

3"

wrong side

bottom hem

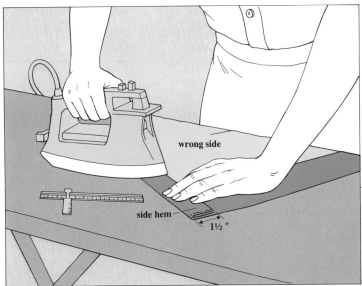

wrong side

side hem

1½"

2 **Folding the bottom hem.** Place the fabric wrong side up on an ironing board or a table suitably padded for ironing. With a hemming gauge, measure 3 inches up from the bottom along one side edge, fold the fabric over at that place, and press the fold with a steam iron set for permanent press. Continue to fold and press along that line, measuring every few inches, until you have creased a fold all the way across the fabric. Then turn up another 3-inch fold to form a double hem (*above*) and press again. Hold the hem in place with pins set at right angles to the hemline.

3 **Preparing the side hems.** Beginning at the bottom hem, measure and turn over a 1½-inch-wide fold along one side, pressing it into place as you move along to the top of the curtain. Then turn the fold again to form a 1½-inch double hem (*above*) and press it down. Pin the hem in place, then repeat the process to press and pin a 1½-inch double hem along the other side of the curtain. ▶

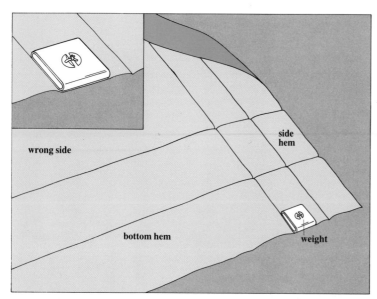

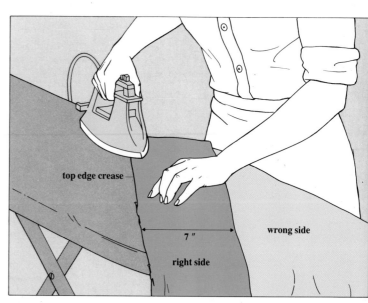

4 **Weighting the hems.** Unpin and unfold the bottom and side hems at the lower corners of the panel. Place a flat, inch-square lead weight at the fabric's bottom edge in the inner fold of each side hem, as seen above. (If your fabric is opaque rather than lace or sheer, see the box at lower right for an alternative positioning of the weights.) Using a double thread with a knot in the end, sew the center bar of the weight (*inset*) to the curtain fabric with three or four loop stitches. Tie off the thread and cut off the excess. Refold the hems and pin them back in place. Now sew the bottom hem by machine using a blind-hem stitch (*page 23*). Then hand-stitch the side hems (*page 22*).

5 **Making the top folds.** Spread the curtain smooth, right side up. From several points on the lower edge of the bottom hem, measure toward the panel's top the distance you established in Step 1 as the curtain's finished length. Mark the fabric there with pins. Then turn the curtain wrong side up, and fold the top of the fabric over along the pin line. Press the fold, removing the pins as you go (*above*). The resulting crease will be the top edge of the completed curtain. Now unfold the fabric, and fold and press another crease 3½ inches up from the top edge crease. Refold the fabric at the top edge crease, and you should have what amounts to a 3½-inch-wide double hem across the top of the curtain; secure it with pins inserted along its lower fold, perpendicular to the fold line.

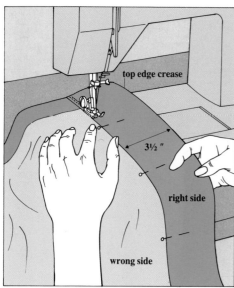

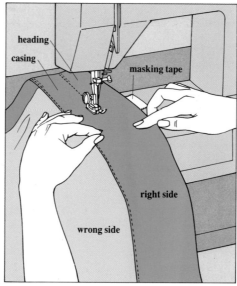

6 **Sewing the casing.** Position the curtain face down on your machine so the needle is over one side edge of the top hem and about ⅛ inch from the hem's bottom edge. Sew about five straight stitches, reverse the machine, then stitch back to where you began; this backstitching will reinforce the corner of the casing. Now sew all the way across the curtain, removing pins as you go. Backstitch again at the end of seam.

7 **Sewing the heading.** Along a side edge, measure 1½ inches up from the casing's bottom seam — sewed in Step 6 — and lower the needle at this point. Place a strip of masking tape on the machine's throat plate along the curtain's top edge. Keep the edge aligned with the tape as you sew across the curtain, backstitching at the beginning and end of the stitching line (*Step 6*). Press the seam. Now make the other curtain by starting again with Step 2.

Weights in Opaque Fabrics

For lace and sheer curtains, weights are placed in the side hems (*Step 4*), where they are hidden by five fabric layers. But in time the weights may pull the side hem into view beneath the edge of the bottom hem. When using an opaque fabric, where two layers will hide the weights, you can avoid that possibility by placing the weights in the bottom hem (*below*).

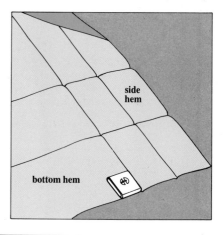

Lined curtains trimmed with bands of color

With only a few additions, you can transform a basic curtain into a luxurious one. Lining will enhance the way a curtain hangs, giving it more body. And a contrasting trim, such as the rose-colored border on the curtains at right, will lend a decorative accent.

Besides adding fullness to a curtain's folds, a lining keeps the face fabric from fading by shielding it from sunlight. Linings also give your windows a uniform appearance from the outside, even if the curtain fabric varies from room to room. Furthermore, the double thickness of fabric and lining absorbs more sound and is a better insulator than an unlined curtain. (To increase a curtain's insulating properties even more, you can add a third layer called an interlining, as demonstrated on pages 48-51, or use one of several specially treated fabrics known as insulating linings.)

In these curtains, the lining extends up the front of the rod casing to the top of the curtain panel and is held in place by the seam that closes the bottom of the casing. The lining's hemmed bottom hangs loose, 1 inch above the bottom of the curtain hem. The side edges of the lining are sewed into the curtain's side hems.

Be sure to choose curtain fabric that is lightweight or medium-weight. A heavy fabric will bunch up on the rod. To determine the amount of fabric needed, take measurements after you have hung the rod *(Steps 1-2, next page)*. A pair of curtains with deep folds requires a total breadth of fabric approximately equal to three times the rod's length. To obtain this expanse, you may have to piece together a number of selvage-to-selvage widths. Step 2 explains how to do this.

After the widths are sewed together, a bottom hem is pressed into place before the large piece is cut into two separate curtain panels; the hem will prevent you from mixing up the ends or side edges of the panels as you proceed with subsequent steps. After a large piece is divided in two, the panels are transposed so that the narrower widths of fabric will hang farthest from the center of the window; there the seams will be easily concealed in the curtain folds. If it takes an even number of fabric widths to make up the whole breadth required, then, of course, half are allotted to each curtain and the widths are sewed as two separate panels.

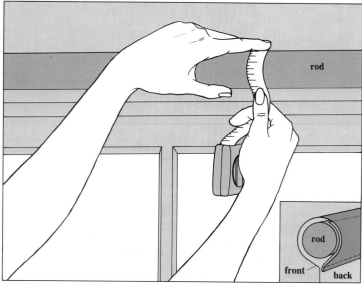

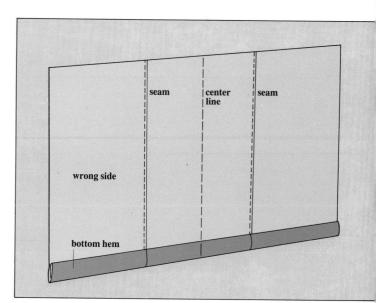

1 **Establishing the curtain's length.** Determine the length of fabric needed for the front of the rod casing by measuring halfway around the curtain rod with a steel tape and adding ½ inch so the fabric will gather easily along the rod. Then add the distance from the bottom of the rod to the floor; subtract ½ inch so the curtain clears the floor. The sum is the length of the finished curtain. To calculate the length of fabric necessary to make a curtain that long, add 8 inches for a 4-inch double bottom hem, and twice the casing length to allow for a double layer of fabric at the back of the casing *(inset).*

2 **Getting the right width.** Multiply the rod's length by three. Figure how many widths of fabric you need for a panel that wide, rounding off to the nearest whole number. Cut those pieces to the length determined in Step 1; Allow for an extra repeat to match patterned fabric *(pages 18-19).* If you have an odd number of widths, as here, pin and sew them together with ½-inch seam allowances. Clip any selvages at 3-inch intervals so they will not pull the fabric if they shrink, and press the seam allowances to one side. Then press in a 4-inch double bottom hem. Open it, fold the piece in half lengthwise and pull a thread at the fold. Cut along that center line to create two panels. Pin the bottom hems in place. If you start with an even number of widths, sew them into two panels.

4 **Folding the side hems.** Turn one curtain at a time wrong side up, then press the trim's seam allowance over the darker-colored fabric to prevent the allowance from showing through when the curtain is hanging.

Refold the curtain's bottom hem and pin it again, this time incorporating the trim into the folds and pressing the folds there in place. Starting from the bottom, measure and fold a double 1½-inch hem at each side of the curtain, pressing the hem flat as you go *(right);* then pin these hems in place. Now stitch curtain weights into the bottom hems next to the side hems *(page 34).*

Finally, sew the bottom hem in place with a blind-hem machine stitch *(page 23, Step 2)* starting and stopping at the inner edges of the side hems; use different threads to match curtain and trim color, tying off one thread when you change to the other.

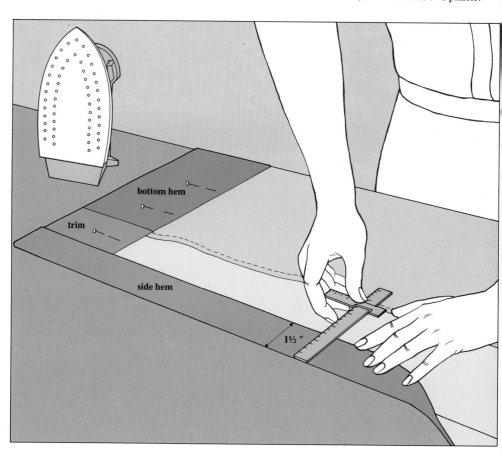

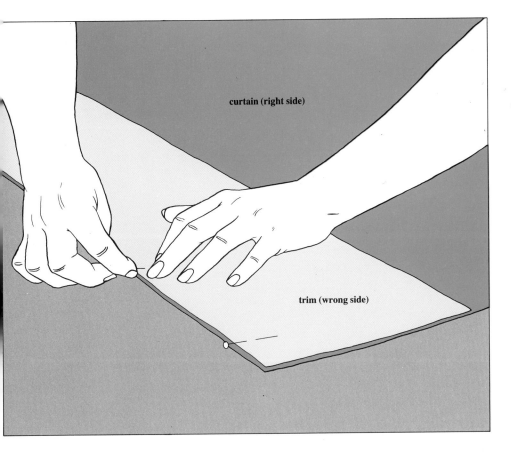

curtain (right side)

trim (wrong side)

3 **Adding the trim.** Decide how wide you want the finished trim to be — 3 inches in this instance. Then add 3 inches for a double 1½-inch side hem, plus ½ inch for a seam allowance. Thus, in this case, the cut width of the trim fabric will be 6½ inches. Square the trim fabric *(page 18),* cut off one of its selvages, and measure and cut two strips of the required width and as long as the total length of the curtain fabric.

Now place a curtain panel right side up on the worktable. Unpin and unfold the bottom hem and place a strip of trim face down on the fabric, aligned with what will be the curtain's leading edge — the edge that will hang toward the center of the window. Pin the trim to the curtain ½ inch from the edge, with the pins at right angles to the edge *(left).* Using a straight stitch, sew a seam along the pin line, removing the pins as they approach the machine's needle. Now attach the other strip of trim to the leading edge of the other curtain.

From this point on, each curtain and its attached trim are treated together as a unit when hemming, attaching lining, creating the rod casing and so forth.

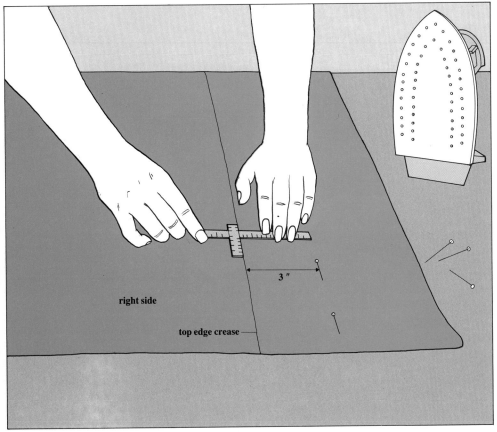

right side

top edge crease

3 "

5 **Measuring for the casing.** Lay each panel in turn right side up on a flat surface. From the bottom, measure off the curtain's finished length and mark that line with pins across the curtain. Fold the fabric under along the pin line, and crease the fold with an iron, removing the pins as you proceed.

Unfold the fabric. Measure from that crease — the top edge crease — toward the top of the fabric the amount required for one layer of the back of the casing (here, 3 inches: 2½ inches for half the rod's circumference plus ½ inch for gathers). Pin, fold under and crease that line as you did the other. The fabric above that crease will be folded under at the back of the casing. ▶

6 **Sewing the lining's hem.** The lining's finished length should be 1 inch shorter than the finished curtain; to find the lining fabric's cut length, add to its finished length 4 inches for a 2-inch double bottom hem. The lining fabric's total width should be equal to that of both finished curtains, with 2 inches added to allow for mistakes in fitting.

Measure, cut and join lengths of lining fabric, as you did curtain fabric in Step 2, to create a piece of the desired width and length (if you wish, you can easily rip lining to size instead of cutting it). If the lining is insulated, be sure the coated side will face the window. Clip across the selvages and press the seam allowances to one side.

Then fold a 2-inch double hem in the bottom and press it. Employing a straight stitch, sew the hem ⅛ inch from the edge (*right*). Press the hem flat, fold the lining in half and cut or tear the cloth along the center line to obtain two pieces.

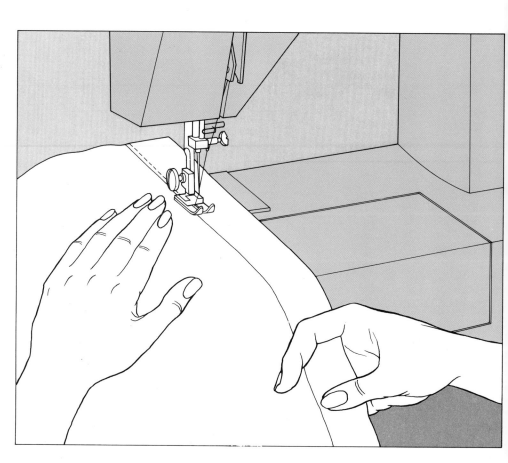

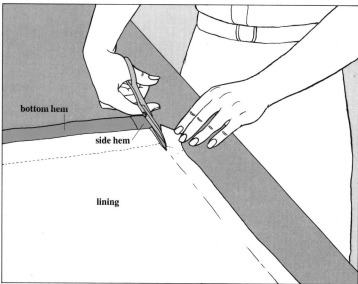

8 **Trimming the lining to the proper width.** Smooth the lining over the entire panel and trim off the portion that extends beyond the second side hem (*above*). Then unpin and turn back that hem and slide the lining against the crease; trim the lining further if necessary for fit. Fold the hem back over the lining and pin it in place. Now position the second lining panel on the other curtain and trim it to fit.

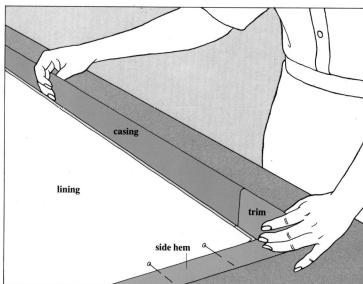

9 **Pinning the lining into the casing.** With each curtain in turn face down and the top of the lining aligned with the top edge crease of the curtain, turn the folds of the back of the casing down over the lining (*above*). Secure the bottom edge of the casing with pins that pass through all four layers of fabric — the two that form the back of the casing, the lining, and the fabric of the curtain's face.

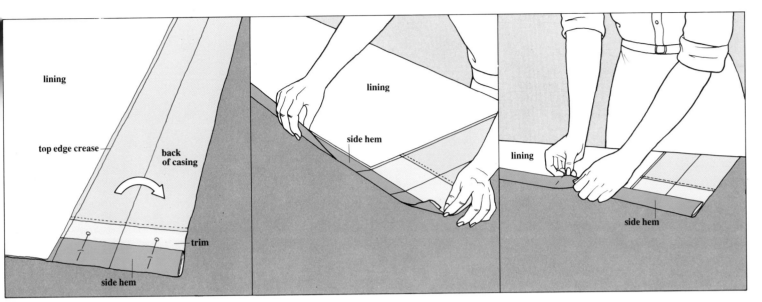

7 **Positioning the lining.** Spread a curtain wrong side up on a flat surface, and turn back the casing fold. Place the lining — the side with the hem fold facing down — on the curtain. Align the lining's top edge and one side with the top edge crease and one side of the curtain *(above, left)*. Remove the pins from that side hem, turn back one fold and insert the lining *(above, center)*. Now turn the hem fold back down, over the lining, and pin the hem with the lining enclosed back in place *(above, right)*.

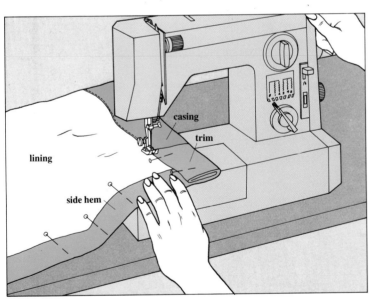

10 **Sewing the rod casing.** Turn a curtain wrong side up and place its upper end on the sewing machine. Beginning by backstitching (sewing about five stitches in reverse to reinforce the end of the seam), sew a straight-stitch seam across the casing, about ⅛ inch from the casing's bottom edge. Remove pins as the needle approaches them. When you reach the trim, tie your thread by stitching in the same place and change to a thread that matches the trim. Tie the new thread, sew to the curtain's edge, then backstitch again.

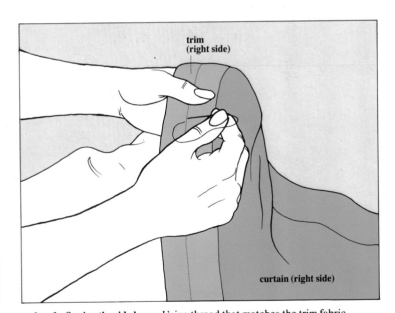

11 **Sewing the side hems.** Using thread that matches the trim fabric along one edge of the curtain and the curtain fabric along the opposite edge, blind-stitch *(page 22)* both side hems of both curtains. About every 5 inches, sew through to the face and reinsert the needle almost where it emerges *(above)* to hold all the fabric layers in place. Make tiebacks *(pages 79-86)*, then hang the curtains.

Some rods — including the one for this curtain — are supported by brackets that protrude in front of the rod *(page 27, top)*. To prevent brackets from interfering with a curtain's casing, fit the curtain on the rod as it should hang; clip a few stitches in the bottom seam of the casing at each bracket. Slip the brackets through the openings.

A scalloped treatment that stays put

Stretch curtains held tight between a pair of stationary rods will provide privacy and ornament while running close to the glass, where they are safe from catching in the frame or blowing in the wind. The curtains' tautness makes them the practical choice for glass-paneled doors, swinging casements and many a sash window in kitchens and bathrooms. Any color, any print can be used; the fabric can be gathered at top and bottom onto rods that slip through casings, or it can be hung in folds from rings, as shown below. Here, scalloped hems give the curtains added interest.

Not only are scallops decorative, but they make it possible to produce curtains with half the usual fabric width: Instead of equaling three times the curtain rod's length, the fabric should be just one and one half times as wide as the rod to prevent the scallops from drooping.

The scallop design is not the exclusive province of stretch curtains, of course. It could just as easily ornament the top edge of short café curtains or full-length draperies, where it would have the same fabric-saving results.

For scalloped stretch curtains the choice of fabric depends on the window's function. Sheer and semisheer fabrics suit windows that are intended to let in light. But where light can be shut out, an opaque, rigid fabric, such as linen or sailcloth, will give the scallops a crisper look.

Before you can estimate how much fabric you will need, you must install the top rod and make a pencil mark at the approximate location for the bottom rod. Then measure the distances between the two rods and the two ends of the top rod to establish the curtain's final dimensions. Only later, when the curtain is completed and suspended from the rings, should you fasten the bottom rod. Mounted this way, the curtain will fall smoothly between the rods without the risk of slacking or pulling too tightly.

Plotting the scallops calls for some basic arithmetic and an ordinary drawing compass (Step 3). When planning your design, you may want to sketch out the spacing and size of the scallops on a strip of paper first, then transfer the pattern onto the fabric. Or you can draw directly on the curtain material with tailor's chalk or a pencil.

Developing a paper pattern is particularly useful when you want to make the same scallops for several curtains of varying widths. To avoid ending with a partial scallop, adjust each curtain's width slightly, tallying the number of full scallops needed on a width that covers the window about one and one half times.

After you have plotted the scalloped edges, you can sew them by machine; the only hand stitching required is for the side hems and for attaching the rings between the scallops. The curtains are ready to hang when the rings are in place.

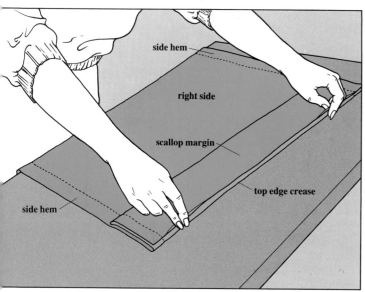

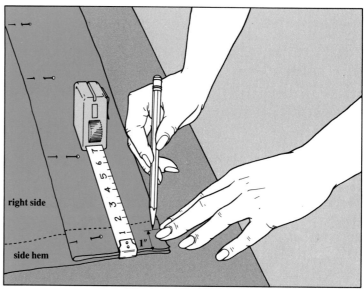

1 **Making the scallop margin.** To establish the length of your curtain, measure the distance between the installed top rod and the location for the bottom rod; subtract ½ inch for curtain rings, but add 16 inches for two 4-inch double hems at top and bottom. To determine the curtain width, multiply the width of the rod by one and one half. Square the fabric *(pages 18-19)* and cut the curtain to these dimensions. Next, fold and press in 1½-inch double side hems and 4-inch double hems at top and bottom *(page 33, Steps 2-3)*. To form a margin for cutting scallops, open the fold of the top hem at the top edge crease and turn back the fabric on that line, right side of fabric to right side *(above)*. Pin the fold of this margin in place. Turn back the opposite end in the same manner.

2 **Planning the scallops.** Fold the curtain in half lengthwise to find the center line, and mark the top and bottom edges there with a pencil. Unfold the curtain, measure 1 inch in from each side of the scallop margin and make a mark *(above)*. Then measure the remaining width and estimate the number of scallops you can make. Scallops should have a diameter of 4 to 6 inches. The spaces between the scallops — one fewer is needed than scallops — should be between ½ and 1 inch. Thus, for seven scallops you should allot six spaces, here 1 inch wide. Deduct that number from the remaining width. In this case the width is 41 inches; subtracting 6 leaves 35 inches. Divide that figure by the number of scallops; the result here will be seven scallops, each 5 inches in diameter.

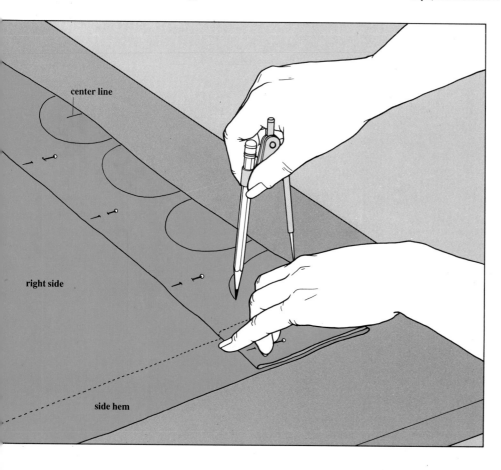

3 **Drawing the curves.** Set a compass at 2½ inches — half the diameter of a scallop — and place its point on the previously marked center line of the curtain. With the pencil point, draw a half circle on the fabric. Mark off 1 inch from one side of the half circle and place the pencil point there; set the compass point 2½ inches away and draw the next half circle. Alternate 1-inch spaces and 5-inch half circles to one edge, then draw in circles and spaces from the center to the opposite edge. Repeat the steps for scallops at the bottom hem. ▶

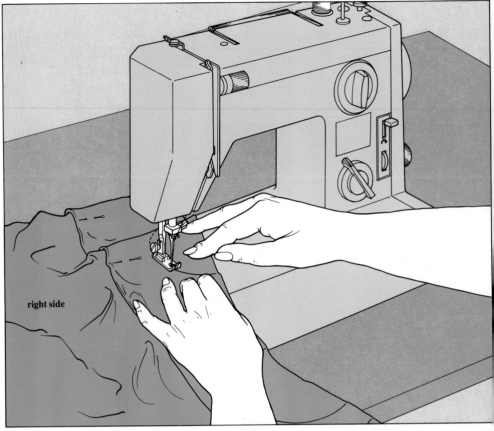

4 **Sewing the scallops.** Set your sewing machine for a medium-length straight stitch — about 10 stitches to the inch. To reinforce the seam, backstitch *(page 34, Step 6)* at one top-crease edge of the first scallop. Then sew along the line to the other edge of the scallop. Backstitch, cut the thread and move on to the next scallop, until all of the half circles are sewed.

right side

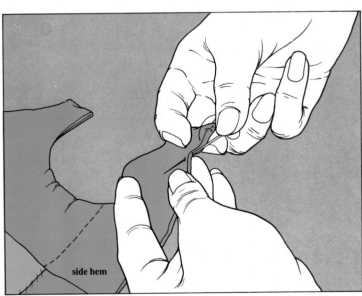

side hem

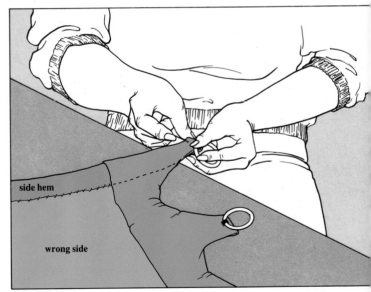

side hem

wrong side

7 **Hand-stitching the scallop margin.** Use a needle with a single thread knotted at the end. Push the needle through a top corner of the scallop margin and pull the thread through; this will hide the knot between the folds of the margin. Blind-stitch *(page 22)* the side of the margin *(above)*. With the same stitch, sew the margin's hem and repeat the steps for the other margin. Finally, blind-stitch the curtain's side hems.

8 **Attaching the rings.** Choose rings about ¼ inch larger than the circumference of your curtain rod. Midway between each pair of scallops sew on a ring, using doubled thread knotted at the end and stitching only to the back of the curtain. Anchor the knot in the fabric, then pass the needle through the ring, stitch into the fabric and through the ring repeatedly until you have looped the thread about five times. To tie a knot, pass the needle back through the loop of the thread and pull it tight; repeat the motion two or three times. Cut the thread and sew on the next ring.

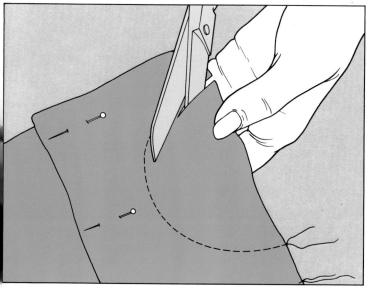

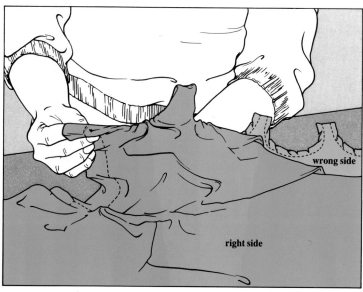

5 **Cutting the scallops.** With sharp scissors, cut around the scallops' seam line, leaving a ¼-inch allowance inside the seam *(above)*. Clip into the seam allowance at right angles to the seam about every ¼ inch, to release the fabric so you can turn the curves inside out without puckering.

6 **Adjusting the scallops.** Turn the scallop margin inside out, pushing out the shaped tops between scallops with your fingers. If a curve does not bend smoothly, clip more of the seam inside. If a corner stays inverted, use a pin to pull it out from the right side. Press the scallops flat.

9 **Locating the bottom rod.** Thread the curtain rings onto the top rod and lock the rod into its brackets. Then fit the bottom rod through its rings and use the rod as a guide to mark the final locations of the brackets. Install the brackets and the rod.

A ruffled, double-faced style

Hung from hinged rods, ruffled curtains present an attractive face whether swung across the window for privacy or away from it for brighter light. To achieve such an effect, the design below calls for two pairs of fabric panels sewed together right side in and then turned right side out. Curving the bottom corners where the curtains meet softens their lines — an effect accentuated by ruffles around the edges and a ruffle-like heading.

Swinging rods in many styles and finishes were common in drapery-laden Victorian homes. Today, however, they often must be specially ordered. But you will have no trouble finding metal holdbacks to draw the lower third of the curtains back from the center of the window

and give them curvaceous outlines; such hardware is widely available in all sorts of styles wherever curtain supplies are sold.

For this type of curtain, a firm, lightweight linen, cotton or cotton blend yields crisp ruffles but does not overtax the hinged rod as a heavier fabric would. The front and back panels of each curtain may be made of a single fabric or of two different fabrics having contrasting patterns or colors. When considering fabrics with different patterns, try out swatches at the window to be sure one fabric does not show through the other in strong light.

To calculate the width of each curtain panel, multiply the length of the rod by two. Add 1 inch for the side seams, then subtract 2½ inches — the width of the finished ruffle. To calculate the panel's

length, measure the height of the window from the top of the casement to the inner sill or, for an outside application, from the top of the window frame to the sill. As before, add an inch for the seams and subtract 2½ inches for the ruffle.

The ruffle is made from a strip of fabric about twice as long as the curved edge of the panel. This long strip consists of short sections cut on the straight grain of the fabric and sewed end to end. For each connecting seam, add 1 inch to the total length needed. Sections cut 6 inches wide will yield a finished ruffle 2½ inches wide.

A casing 2½ inches from the top edge of the curtain creates the ruffle-like heading. The depth of the casing should be one and a half times the diameter of the rod.

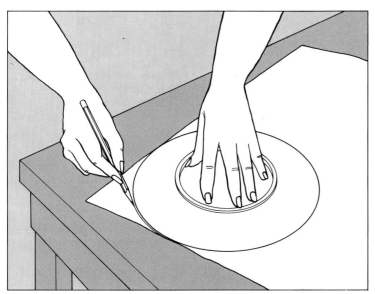

1 **Making a pattern.** From a sheet of heavy paper cut an 18-inch square. Place a plate 10 or 12 inches in diameter face down on a corner of the paper so that the plate's edge meets two adjacent sides of the square. Draw a curve by tracing the outline of the plate from one side of the square to the other. Remove the plate and, using the traced outline as a guide, cut off the corner of the paper. Adjust the degree of curve if desired.

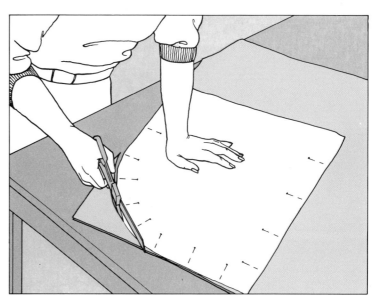

2 **Cutting the curve in the fabric.** Square the curtain fabric *(page 18),* then cut two panels of the required length and width for each curtain, matching the pattern from one curtain to the other *(page 19).* Lay one panel atop the other, right sides together and edges aligned. Place the pattern on the fabric with its curve at one corner. Align the edges of the pattern and the panels, then pin the pattern in place. Following the curve, cut both panels together. Measure the length of the entire curved edge, from the corner of one adjacent side to the corner of the other, and double this distance to determine the length of the fabric strip needed for the ruffle. Unpin the pattern and set the panels aside.

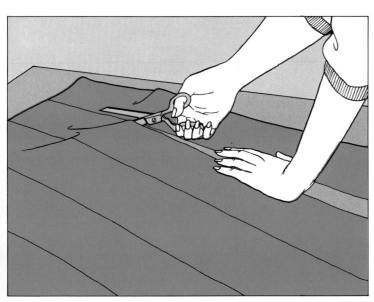

3 **Cutting the ruffle.** Measure 6 inches from the cut end of a squared length of fabric and use chalk to mark a line, from selvage to selvage. Along one selvage, measure 6 inches from the line and mark again; repeat until you have enough sections to make up the length of the ruffle plus seam allowances. Cut the sections apart along the chalk lines.

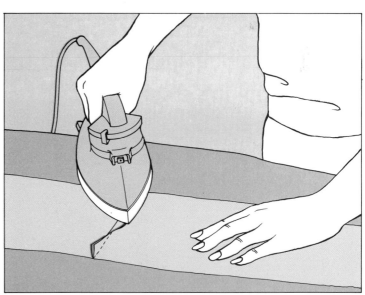

4 **Joining the ruffle sections.** Place one ruffle section atop another, right sides together, and pin them at one end. Using a straight machine stitch, eight to the inch, sew across the pinned end, leaving a ½-inch seam allowance. Connect the remaining sections in the same fashion to make one long strip. Press all the seam allowances to one side *(above).* ▶

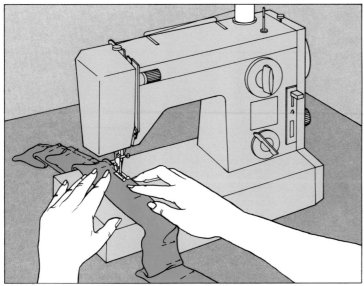

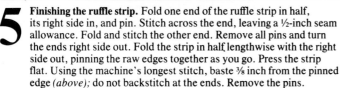

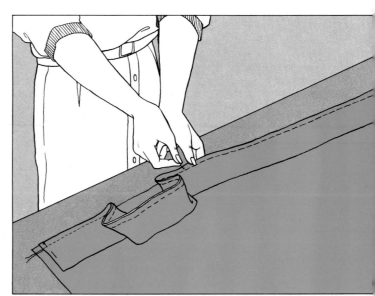

5 **Finishing the ruffle strip.** Fold one end of the ruffle strip in half, its right side in, and pin. Stitch across the end, leaving a ½-inch seam allowance. Fold and stitch the other end. Remove all pins and turn the ends right side out. Fold the strip in half lengthwise with the right side out, pinning the raw edges together as you go. Press the strip flat. Using the machine's longest stitch, baste ⅜ inch from the pinned edge *(above)*; do not backstitch at the ends. Remove the pins.

6 **Pinning the ruffle strip to the panel.** Align the basted edge of the ruffle strip with the curved edge of the right side of the front panel. Pin one end of the strip ½ inch from the top corner of the panel. Measure 20 inches from that end of the strip, insert a pin, and anchor it to the panel 10 inches from the first pin: The basted edge of the ruffle strip should be even with the panel's edge. Continue measuring 20-inch lengths and pinning them to the panel at 10-inch intervals. Pin the end of the strip ½ inch from the second corner of the panel.

9 **Joining the back and front panels.** Make a chalk mark on the right side of the back panel so you will be able to distinguish it from the front panel later. Lay the back panel on the front panel, with the right sides together and the ruffle sandwiched between them. Align the edges of the panels, then pin them together *(right)*. Stitch around the sides and bottom of the panel ½ inch from the edge, but leave a 10-inch opening at the top. Turn the curtain right side out through the opening. Press the edges flat; avoid pressing the ruffle. Close the opening by hand, using an overcast stitch *(page 22)*.

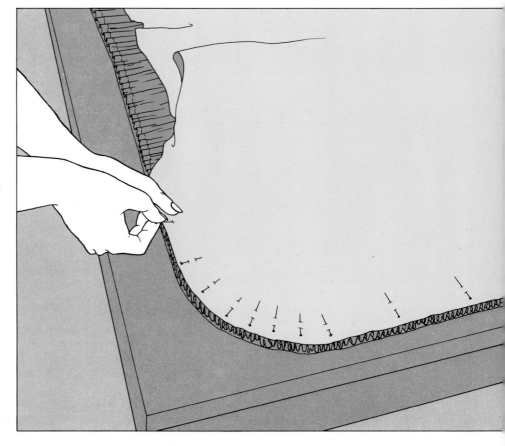

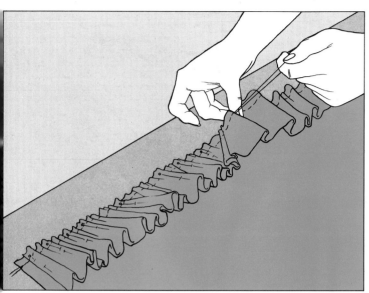

7 **Gathering the ruffle.** With the tip of a seam ripper or the blunt side of a scissors blade, lift up a basting-stitch thread from the ruffle strip, about halfway between two pins. Pull the loop of thread with the fingers of one hand; with the other hand, work the ruffle gathers evenly along the length of strip between the pins. If necessary, pull up one or two more loops of thread to even the gathers. When the ruffle strip is gathered sufficiently to lie flat against the panel, pin them together, making sure their edges are aligned. Continue to gather and pin the ruffle, section by section, easing it around the curved part of the panel edge.

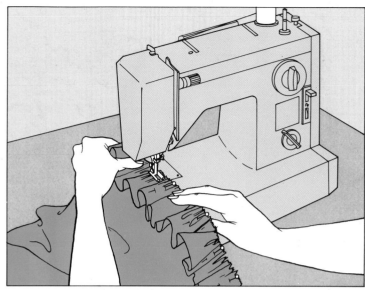

8 **Sewing the ruffle to the panel.** Insert the panel and ruffle under the presser foot, ruffle side up. Stitch ⅜ inch from the edge, removing each pin from the fabric just before it reaches the needle. Then lay the panel flat on the worktable, ruffle side up.

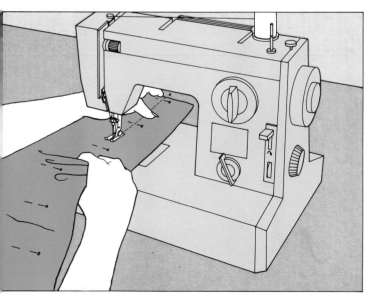

10 **Making the rod casing.** Insert pins across the top of the curtain to hold the panels together securely. Stick a piece of masking tape onto the sewing-machine throat plate 2½ inches from the needle and set the stitch length at eight to the inch. Using the masking tape as a guide, stitch straight across the curtain, creating a heading 2½ inches high. Remove the pins and stitch another line parallel to the first, set far enough below it to hold the rod.

11 **Finishing the rod casing.** Using a seam ripper or embroidery scissors, snip open the ends of the rod casing between the two lines of stitching. On the ruffle edge, snip only the stitches that are visible on the back panel; do not snip the stitches that hold the ruffle to the front panel. Hem the openings with an overcast stitch.

The airy opulence of poufs

Pouf — meaning puff — curtains combine the opulence of a formal window treatment with the airiness of a contemporary one. As seen in this photograph, the fabric billows at the pouf, then falls in deep folds that sweep the floor.

The curtains are three times as wide as the area they cover. Because of this fullness — and in order to achieve the billowing effect — the fabric you choose should be fairly lightweight; silk was used for these curtains. A stiff or heavyweight fabric would not gather easily along the rod or at the shirring tape that helps to create the pouf.

To reinforce the curtains, a cotton flannel interlining fits between the lining and the curtain fabric *(opposite)*. Both the lining and interlining hang straight; only the curtain fabric puffs out.

The pouf is formed by drawing 10 inches of fabric up into a tuck and sewing shirring tape beneath it. A cloth strip about an inch wide, shirring tape encases two to four cords that parallel the length of the tape. Pulling the cords shirrs, or gathers, the curtain beneath the pouf.

Available in fabric stores, shirring tape comes in white or ecru; a double-stranded tape is used here.

Additional poufs can easily be incorporated into each curtain: Add an extra 10 inches of fabric to the length of the curtain for each pouf when calculating yardage and follow Steps 4 and 5 *(pages 50-51)* to create each pouf.

A lined sleeve gathered onto the rod between the two curtains unites the window treatment. When using a patterned fabric like this, with vertical swaths of different hues, the material for the sleeve

could be cut across the fabric's width, so the sleeve would mirror the colors of the curtains. Here, however, the sleeve was cut lengthwise from the fabric to provide a solid-colored contrast.

Instructions for determining the length of curtain fabric, lining and interlining are given below. Step 2 on page 36 explains how to calculate and assemble the total width of fabric. But remember that a sleeve encases the rod between the curtains: To figure fabric width, measure only those parts of the rod the finished curtains will cover.

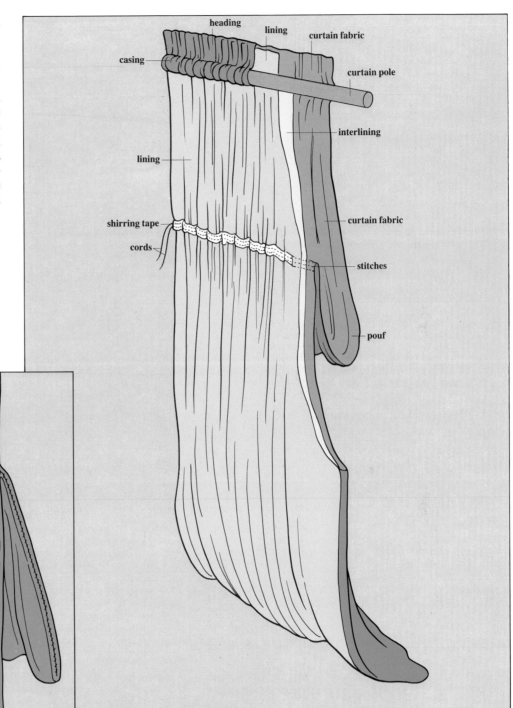

Anatomy of a pouf curtain. The pouf curtain seen from the back in this cutaway diagram is lined and interlined. The lining, which falls 1 inch short of the bottom of the curtain, passes around the front of the rod and fits inside the heading — the fabric that extends above the rod. The interlining is sandwiched between the lining and the curtain fabric; its top edge is sewed into the bottom of the rod casing, and its bottom edge is inserted into the bottom hem of the lining.

The pouf is formed by 10 inches of curtain fabric hiked up into a loose tuck. It is held in place by stitching that secures the fabric just below the top of the tuck to the interlining, lining and a shirring tape — a fabric strip with pull cords. The cords are pulled to gather the curtain and make the loose fabric balloon into a pouf. The sides of the pouf are sewed closed *(inset)*.

The curtain's finished length is the sum of the height of the heading, half of the rod circumference plus ½ inch so the curtain gathers easily *(page 36, Step 1),* the distance from the rod to the floor, 10 inches for the pouf and another 10 inches for the fabric draped onto the floor. For the total fabric length required, add to the finished length 8 inches for a 4-inch double hem at the bottom, and twice the amount already allowed for the heading and the rod; this last amount will provide the large double hem that forms the back of the heading and casing.

To determine the length of lining fabric, subtract 10 inches from the curtain's finished length because the lining has no pouf and 1 inch because it is shorter than the curtain; then add 4 inches for a double 2-inch hem. For the interlining, measure from the bottom of the rod to the floor; add ½ inch to be sewed into the casing and 9 inches to sweep the floor.

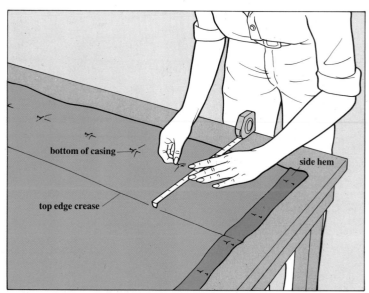

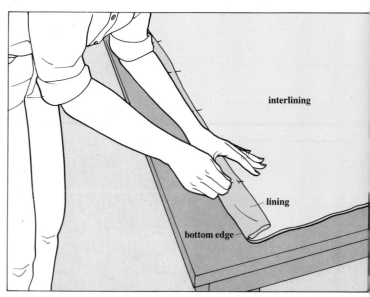

1 **Establishing the top fold.** Use the technique in Step 2, page 36, to cut two curtains; follow Steps 2-4, pages 33-34, to sew in bottom hems and pin side hems. Then lay each curtain in turn wrong side up. At 6-inch intervals, measure the curtain's finished length up from the bottom and insert pins. Fold at the pin line and iron in a crease, then unfold the fabric and remove the pins. Measure up from that crease — the top edge crease — the length of one layer of casing and heading (here, 6 inches: 3 inches for the heading, 2½ inches for half the rod's circumference and ½ inch for gathering the curtain). Mark this line with pins *(above)*, fold the fabric there, iron in a crease and remove the pins. The fabric above the last crease will be folded under behind the casing and heading.

2 **Assembling the lining and interlining.** Cut the lining and interlining to the lengths determined on page 49, producing enough pieces of each kind of fabric to yield a total width equal to the combined width of both curtain panels with side hems in place, plus 2 inches to allow for mistakes in fitting. Sew and cut the pieces to form two interlining panels and two lining panels *(page 38, Step 6)*. Fold a 2-inch double hem in the bottom of each lining panel and press it with an iron. Open the hem and position one end of an interlining panel at the crease that will be the bottom edge of the hemmed lining. Align the side edges of the lining and interlining, fold the lining's doubled bottom hem over the interlining, and pin the hem in place *(above)*.

4 **Placing the pouf.** Decide where on the window you want the curtain to puff out; in the photograph on page 48 the pouf falls just above the window's meeting rail. Measure from that point on the window to the floor and add 10 inches for the fabric that will sweep the floor. Lay each curtain in turn wrong side up on a flat surface. From the bottom of the curtain, measure the required distance and mark it with a row of pins across the curtain. Measure 10 inches from that row of pins toward the top of the curtain, and mark that distance with a second row of pins *(right)*.

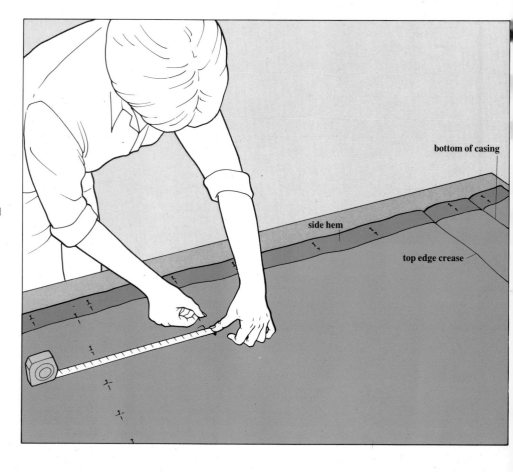

3 **Lining and interlining.** Smooth the interlining toward the top of each lining panel and pin the two sections together at the top of the interlining. Along a line ¼ inch down from the interlining's top edge, baste the two panels together by hand *(right)*, using a single thread knotted at the end: Start about ¼ inch from a side edge and make each basting stitch about ½ inch long *(inset)*. Do not pull the stitches so tight that they cause the fabric to pucker.

When you reach the other side edge, clip the thread and remove the pins from the basted seam. Then, using a straight stitch on the sewing machine, sew the lining's bottom hem in place, removing the pins as they approach the machine's needle.

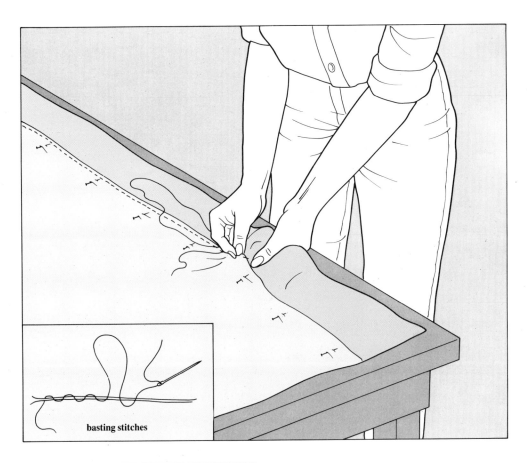

basting stitches

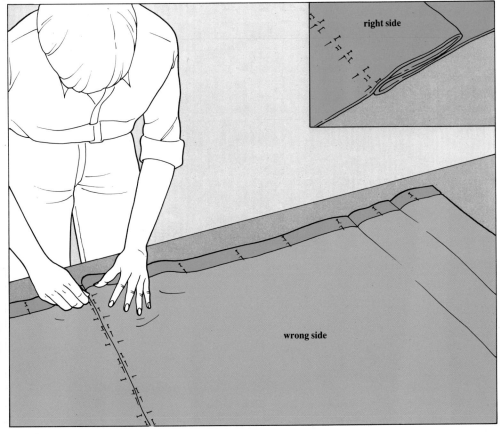

right side

wrong side

5 **Pinning the pouf.** Lift the fabric at the row of pins closest to the top of the curtain, bring that row down to meet the lower row of pins, and form the tuck that will create the pouf. Smooth out the tuck toward the curtain's top. Pin the fold in place across the panel, placing the pins of this row perpendicular to the previous two rows *(left)*.

Now turn the fabric right side up and pin the same fold in place on the curtain's face *(inset)*, pointing the pins toward the bottom hem so that their heads will not interfere with the sewing machine's needle later, when you sew the shirring tape in place *(Step 9)*. Turn the curtain wrong side up once more and remove the three rows of pins marking the pouf on that side. ▶

6 **Pinning on the lining.** Taking each curtain in turn, lay the lining and interlining on the curtain fabric, with the interlining resting against the curtain fabric's wrong side. Align the top and side edges of the lining with the top edge crease and the side edges of the curtain. Fold the top of the curtain at the creases made in Step 1; the double-folded fabric should just cover the basting stitches on the lining. If not, turn back the fold of fabric, shift the lining upward until the stitches can be covered, and trim any excess lining that extends beyond the curtain fabric's top edge crease.

Then, handling the lining and interlining as if they were a single layer, fold them under at the sides so the folded edge is 1 inch in from the edge of the curtain *(right)*. Pin the lining and interlining to the curtain as you fold them, but do not pin through the part of the curtain fabric that will form the pouf *(inset)*. Now remove the pins inserted earlier to hold the curtain's side hems.

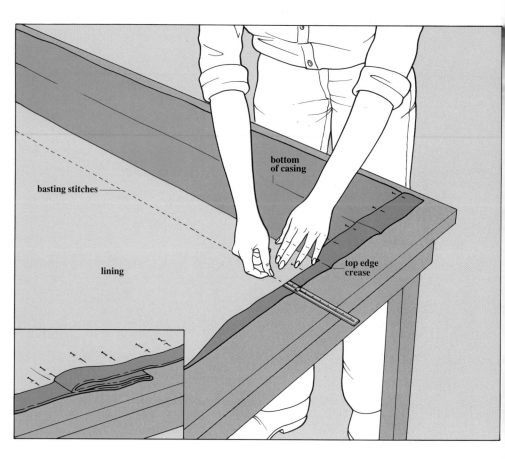

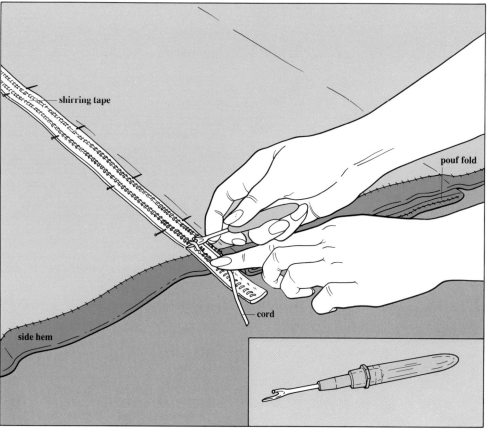

8 **Positioning the shirring tape.** Cut a piece of shirring tape for each curtain, making it 2 inches longer than the width of the curtain panel. Position it across the back of the panel just below the join of the pouf fold, with 1 inch of tape overhanging each side of the curtain. Pin the tape in place.

Use small scissors or a seam ripper *(inset)* to cut the threads encasing the cords where the tape crosses the edge of the lining, and pull the cords free *(left)*. Unpin the tape at the side hem, tuck the extra length of tape underneath, and repin the end of the tape, letting the cords hang free. Now do the same at the other end of the tape.

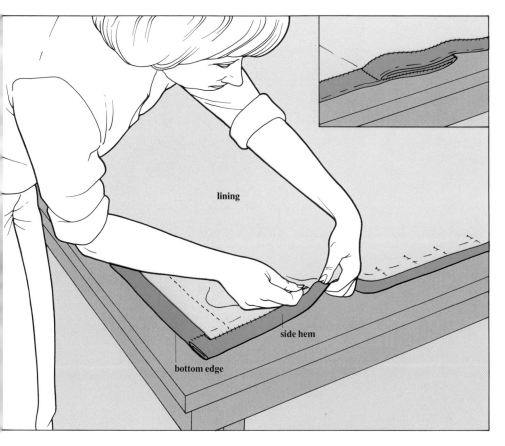

lining

side hem

bottom edge

7 **Hand-stitching the side seams.** Use a blind-hem stitch *(page 22)* to sew each curtain's side hems from the bottom of the panel up to where the lining begins; secure the thread and cut it short.

Reknot the thread and blind-stitch the lining to the curtain on top of each side hem, removing pins as you reach them. About every 5 inches push the needle through to the front of the curtain and bring it back up at almost the same point to tack the fabric layers together. However, do not catch the fold of fabric for the pouf in the stitches.

Next, reknot the thread and stitch together the pouf's sides and the fold across the back of the side hems *(inset)*. Then turn the double fold at the top of the curtain over the lining and pin it in place.

9 **Sewing the shirring tape in place.** To permit the top part of each curtain to pass under the arm of the sewing machine, roll it to within 3 inches of the shirring tape. Make sure the pouf is well out of the way of the machine's needle. Then, backstitching at the beginning and end of each seam *(page 34, Step 6),* sew a straight stitch along each side of the tape about ⅛ inch from the edge. Next, stitch along the center of the tape between the two cords. Now turn the curtain over and remove the pins that held the pouf in place. ▶

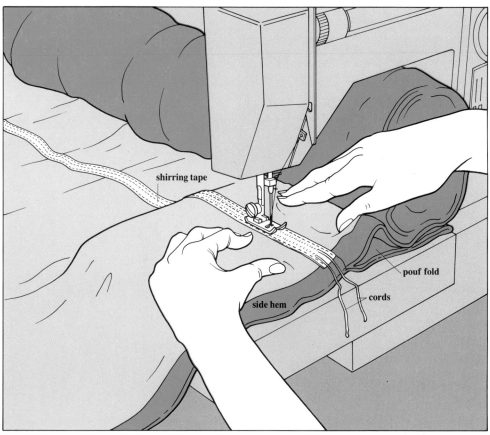

shirring tape

pouf fold

cords

side hem

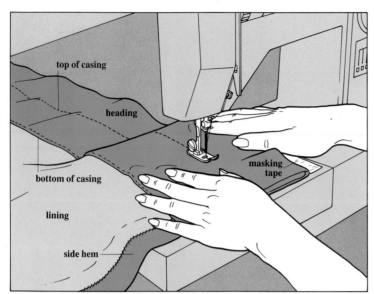

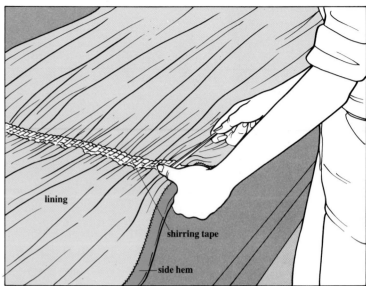

10 **Sewing casing and heading.** Laying each curtain in turn face down on the machine, sew straight across the double fold at the curtain's top, ⅛ inch from its bottom edge; backstitch at the beginning and end of this seam, which closes the casing bottom and secures the interlining. Then lay the curtain face down on a worktable, measure down from the top edge the height of the heading — here, 3 inches — on each side hem and insert a pin parallel to the casing. Position one pin under the machine's presser foot, and put masking tape on the throat plate to mark where the curtain's top edge lies; the tape will guide the fabric. Remove the pins and sew across the panel (above), backstitching at the beginning and end.

11 **Creating the pouf.** Lay each curtain on a flat surface, wrong side up. With one hand, pull the cords of the shirring tape on one side of the curtain; with the other hand, push the fabric along the cords toward the curtain's center. Gather only half of the curtain's finished width at that side of the curtain, and tie the cords together in a knot. Repeat at the other side of the tape to finish gathering the curtain to the desired width, then tie those cords in a bow.

14 **Turning the sleeve right side out.** Slip your hand into the rod sleeve and slide the fabric up onto your arm until you can grasp the other end of the sleeve and pull it right side out. If the sleeve is too narrow for your arm, roll the right side out bit by bit by reaching into the sleeve with your fingers. Then iron the sleeve flat, pressing the seam to the bottom of the sleeve and slightly to the back. Measure down from the top of the sleeve the height of the heading — here, 3 inches. Mark that point with a pin on each end of the sleeve, and follow the instructions in Step 10 to sew the seam with a masking-tape guide.

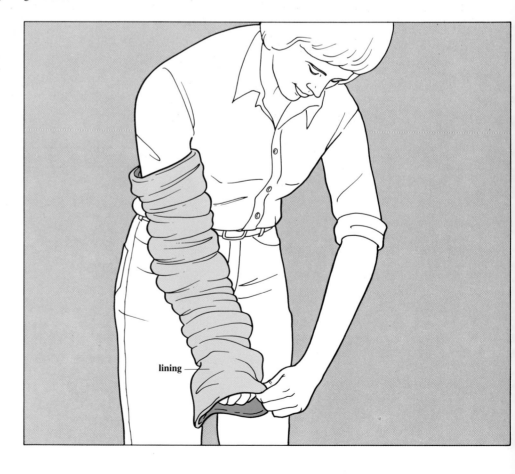

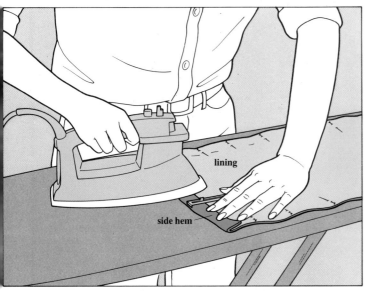

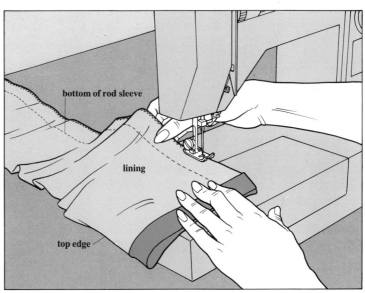

12 **Starting the rod sleeve.** To find the total fabric length for the rod sleeve, start with the circumference of the curtain rod (here, 5 inches). Add 1 inch to allow the sleeve to be gathered on the rod, plus double the height of the heading (in this case, 6 inches), and 2 inches for a seam allowance. The total width of fabric needed is triple the length of the part of the rod that is to be encased. Cut fabric and lining to those dimensions. Lay the fabric on a flat surface wrong side up and align the lining on it; pin the lining in place across the top and bottom of the sleeve fabric. Then measure, fold and press in a double 1-inch hem at each end — the short dimension — of the sleeve. Pin the hems in place and blind-stitch them by hand.

13 **Sewing the sleeve.** Fold the sleeve along its width — the long dimension — with the right sides of the fabric face to face. Sew a straight seam along the entire width 1 inch from the raw edges of the fabric, removing the pins as you come to them. Then overcast the raw seam edges using a machine zigzag stitch *(page 22)*.

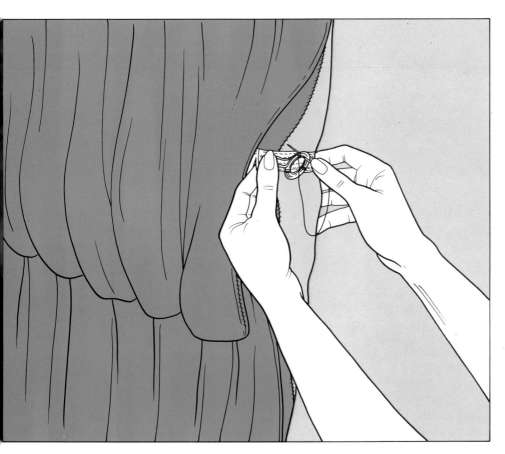

15 **Finishing the job.** Slide the rod sleeve and the curtains onto the rod and hang the rod in place. Adjust curtains and sleeve to their planned positions along the rod. Fluff out the poufs; untie the shirring-cord bow and make any necessary adjustments in the gathers of the curtains, then knot the cords securely.

Now wind the loose ends of each set of cords around two fingers, slip the cord circlet off your fingers and sew it to the shirring tape with loop stitches at several points *(left)*. Finally, arrange the sweeping bottoms of the curtains as if they had fallen naturally onto the floor.

Tab curtains with threaded tiebacks

Crenelated tops and straight, lined folds give these tab curtains a distinctly architectural look. The tabs responsible for the toothed top profile are merely fabric loops, sewed on to hold the curtains to the wood rods. But buckram stiffens the tabs as well as the curtain tops themselves to keep all of their edges equally well squared.

The outside edges of the curtains shown at right hang in straight folds, anchored at the top by drapery hooks looped over tenterhooks *(diagram, right)*. The inner edges are drawn apart in a tieback effect created with rows of small ring hooks, which — like tenterhooks — are available in the drapery section of fabric or department stores. A cord threaded through each set of rings is knotted to a screw eye in the window frame to pull back the curtain's folds.

In this installation, two windows located close to a corner are draped with three curtains: A single central panel extends around the rods on both sides, helping to join the windows and disguise the fact that one is somewhat closer to the corner of the room than the other. Since this is not a typical situation, the instructions on the following pages describe making a pair of curtains to fit a single window. However, the same steps apply to constructing a three-curtain arrangement like the one shown here.

Stapling a wrap of fabric (here, a matching one) to the curtain rods adds polish to the window treatment. As a final touch, the paint used for the brackets and finials, or decorative endpieces, of the rods repeats the dominant color of the curtain fabric.

To hang properly, curtain tabs must slip easily around the rod's circumference, with a 1-inch clearance between the rod and the curtain. They then require enough extra length to fit 1 inch down within the curtain heading so they will be held securely.

Tastes vary, but most curtain makers find a finished width of 1 to 2 inches for the tabs agreeable and prefer medium-weight fabrics such as cotton broadcloth, denim, narrow-wale corduroy or chintz. Lightweight fabrics are too fragile; heavyweight fabrics are bulky and will not lie flat on the rod. For rich effect, the curtains are cut generously — triple the width of the area to be covered — and are lined for extra body.

The tied-back tab curtain. The curtains at left owe their crisp folds to careful engineering on the back side, shown below. The curtain tops and the tabs are reinforced by buckram, hidden inside the curtain fabric. The tabs are inserted between the lining and the curtain fabric, and secured by a seam across the curtain's top. Ring hooks are fastened to the back — through both lining and curtain fabric — in a line slanting up from the curtain's center edge *(below, left side)*. A cord laced through the rings is pulled to tie the curtain back, then knotted at a screw eye on the window frame *(below, right side)*. A tenterhook at the curtain's return edge holds a drapery hook to keep that corner smooth.

1 **Measuring.** To determine the curtain's finished length, measure from the bottom of the curtain rod to the floor. Subtract 1 inch so the curtains do not touch the floor and another inch for space between the curtains and the rod. For the total fabric length, add 4 inches for a single top hem and 8 inches for a double 4-inch bottom hem; the total length of the lining will be 5 inches less than the total fabric length. The curtains' width will be triple the rod's length. Follow Step 2, page 36 to join fabric widths if necessary. For the total tab length, measure the rod's circumference and add 4 inches. For the total tab width, double the finished width — here, 1¾ inches — and add 1 inch for the seam allowance. ▶

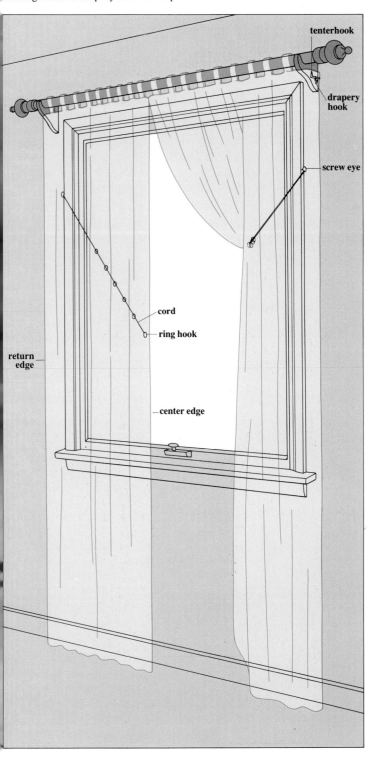

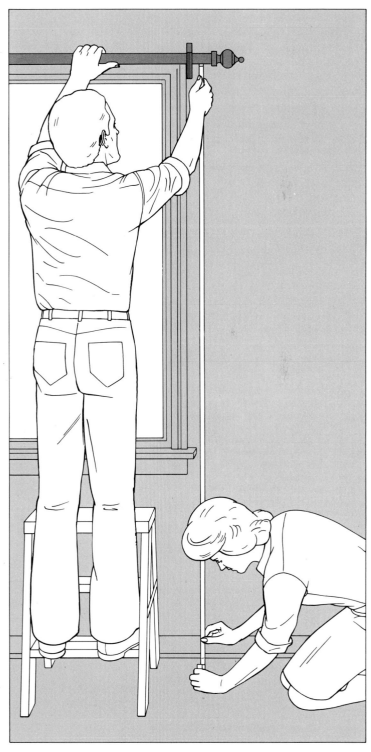

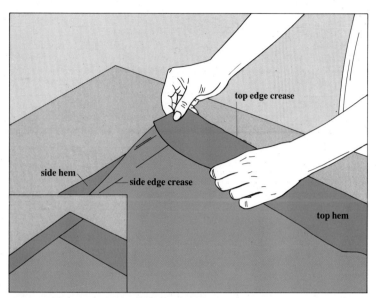

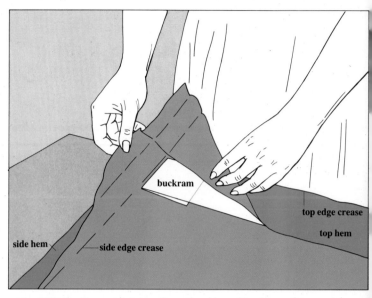

2 **Folding the top and side hems.** Sew the bottom hems and pin the double side hems for two curtains (pages 33-34, Steps 2-4). Then lay one curtain at a time on a flat work surface, wrong side facing upward. Starting from one bottom corner of the curtain, measure the finished length of the curtain along the side and mark it with a pin; continue measuring and pinning at 6-inch intervals across the panel. To make the top hem, fold the fabric on the pin line and crease it with an iron. Now open the hem and remove the pins. Unpin and open an 8-inch length of each side hem at the top of the curtain. Then fold the top hem over once more (above) and refold the side hem over it to hide the raw edge of the top hem (inset). Pin the side hems in place; press with an iron.

3 **Stiffening the curtain's top.** Open the side and top hems of one curtain at a time. Cut a strip of 4-inch-wide buckram 6 inches longer than the width of the curtain. Fold over 3 inches at one end of the buckram, crease the fold and fit the end, folded side down, into a corner of the curtain where the top edge crease and the side edge crease meet (above). Fold the top and side hems over the buckram, and pin the corner. Smooth the buckram across the panel, aligning its upper edge against the top edge crease. Pin the buckram at 6-inch intervals as you proceed. At the opposite side of the curtain, fold the buckram under to fit it into the corner. Fold the top and side hems over the end, and pin the corner.

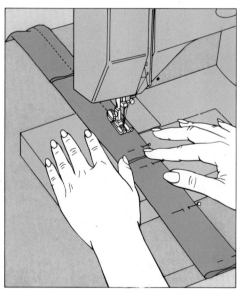

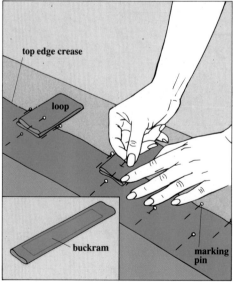

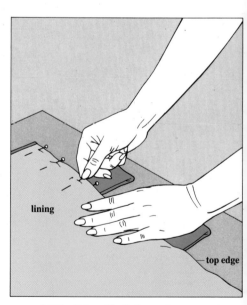

5 **Sewing the tabs.** Cut fabric strips for the tabs to the size determined in Step 1. Fold the strips in half lengthwise, right sides together, and pin. Stitch ½ inch from the raw edges, then — just before the end of the seam — place a second tab end-to-end with the first one. Feed the second tab through without stopping, and repeat the action for the remaining tabs. Clip the threads linking them together, turn the tabs right side out and press them so the seam is at the center.

6 **Pinning tabs to the curtain.** Cut buckram strips 2 inches shorter and ¼ inch narrower than the tabs. Pull a strip through each tab, and center it inside (inset). Fold the tabs in half crosswise, seams together, and press the fold between your fingers. Pin the ends of the tabs 1 inch below the curtain's top edge, at the positions marked in Step 4; direct the pinheads away from the curtain (above). Then remove the pins inserted in Step 3 to hold the top hem.

7 **Adding lining.** Cut lining to the correct length (Step 1). Join pieces so that the lining's total width exceeds both curtains' finished width by 2 inches. Sew a double 2-inch bottom hem. Cut the lining in half lengthwise and press in single 4-inch top hems. Lay each curtain in turn wrong side up and lay the lining atop it; align the top and one side edge. Pin the layers together (above) and trim off the excess lining at the curtain's other side.

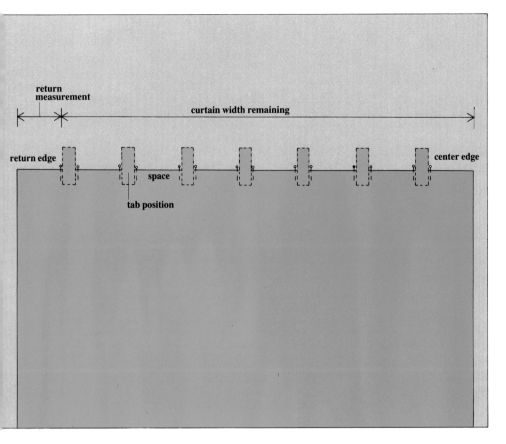

return measurement
curtain width remaining
return edge
center edge
space
tab position

4 **Determining tab placement.** Measure the return — the distance from the front of the curtain rod to the wall. Use a pin to mark that measurement from the outer edge of one curtain at a time. This so-called return edge will curve to cover the return space.

Measure the distance between the pin and the curtain's center edge. Add the return width to the finished tab width and divide this figure into the curtain-width measurement. If necessary, round the return-plus-tab figure up or down slightly until it divides evenly into the curtain-width measurement. The result represents the number of tabs and spaces that the remaining curtain width will accommodate.

To calculate the width of each space, subtract the finished tab width from the adjusted return-plus-tab figure. Starting at the pin that marks the return measurement, measure the width of a tab and insert a pin. Continue marking spaces and tabs across the panel; end with a space.

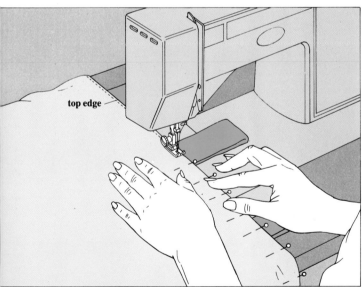

top edge

8 **Sewing the curtain's top edge.** Turn the lining under 1 inch at the side hems, pin it in place and blind-stitch the side hems by hand *(page 22)*. Position the top edge of the curtain, right side facing up, under the presser foot of the sewing machine. Stitch across the curtain ⅛ inch from the edge *(above)*, locking the thread at the beginning and end of the seam *(page 21, bottom)*. Remove the pins as you come to them.

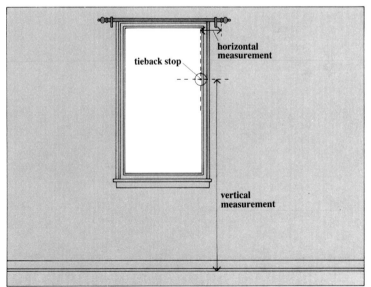

horizontal measurement
tieback stop
vertical measurement

9 **Figuring tieback positions.** Decide how far you want each curtain's center edge to draw back. Mark this point on the window frame with a pencil, or on the window glass with masking tape. Then align a yardstick with the mark and draw one line on the wall out to the rod's end, and another down from the rod's end to intersect the first one. Measure from the mark to the intersection, triple the distance and add the rod return *(Step 4)* for the horizontal measure. For the vertical measure, subtract 1 inch from the floor-to-mark distance. Lay the curtain wrong side up. At the bottom hem, measure in from the return edge the horizontal distance; mark with a pin. From that pin, measure the vertical distance, and mark with a pin. This is where the top ring hook will be placed. ▶

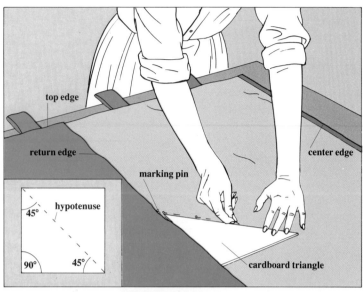

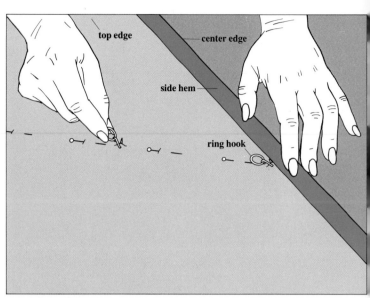

10 **Marking the tieback angle.** Fold the return edge of the curtain over to the marking pin; align the top and bottom of the curtain and smooth it flat. Cut a square piece of firm cardboard corner to corner, forming a right-angled triangle *(inset)*. Lay the triangle on the curtain with one 45° angle touching the marking pin and one side of the right angle flush against the return edge; the hypotenuse of the triangle should slant down toward the center edge. Place pins along the hypotenuse *(above)*. Then align a yardstick with the hypotenuse and continue pinning; end at the side hem of the center edge.

11 **Inserting ring hooks.** Attach ring hooks through the lining and the curtain fabric at the ends of the pin line and at 6-inch intervals between them, directing the point of the hook toward the top edge of the curtain *(above)*. Then, starting at the point on the window or the frame where the curtain's center edge will fall when tied back, measure to the outer edge of the window frame; add 10 inches to that measurement and cut a piece of lightweight nylon cord to that length. Tie the end of the cord to the ring closest to the curtain's center edge, and thread it through the other rings.

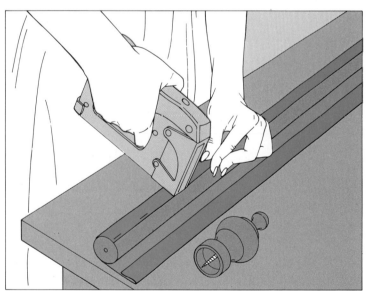

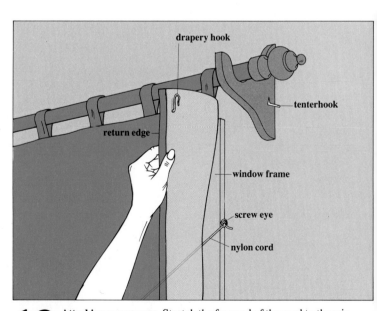

12 **Covering a wood rod with fabric.** Cut fabric to the same length as the rod and 1½ inches wider than the rod's circumference; if you must join fabric pieces to accommodate the rod's length, add ½ inch to each piece joined for each seam required. Fold 1 inch of one long edge of the fabric under and press with an iron. Then lay the fabric flat, wrong side up. Unscrew the finials from the rod and lay it lengthwise on the fabric. Using a staple gun, staple the fabric's long raw edge to the rod. Wrap the fabric snugly around the rod and staple the folded edge over the raw edge. Slip the rod through the curtain tabs, and screw on the finials; they will cover the raw fabric edges at the ends of the rod. Hang the rod and the curtain.

13 **Attaching a screw eye.** Stretch the free end of the cord to the window frame's outer edge, maintaining the 45° angle of the ring hooks. Pencil a tick mark on the frame where the cord crosses it. At the mark, hammer a ½-inch-deep pilot hole with a brad or a small nail. Insert a screw eye that is ½ inch in diameter. Pull the cord to draw the curtain back and tie the cord to the screw eye.

Wrap the curtain's return edge around the rod bracket to cover it. Make a mark on the wall next to the outer edge of the bracket ½ inch below the top edge of the curtain, and tap a tenterhook into the mark. Fasten a drapery hook on the curtain's back close to the top of the return edge and slip it over the tenterhook.

Bow-tied Ribbons

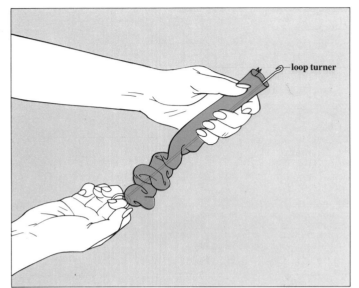

1 **Making ribbons.** Make two curtains, sewing the bottom hems and pinning the top and side hems *(page 58, Step 2)*. Calculate the length and width of each ribbon *(left)*, then determine the number of ribbons needed and mark their positions on the curtain *(page 59, Step 4)*. Cut fabric strips for all the ribbons; next, fold one at a time in half lengthwise, right sides together, and pin it. Sew a straight-stitch seam ¼ inch from the long raw edges *(page 58, Step 5)*. Push a loop turner through the ribbon and catch the end with the turner's hook *(above)*; turn the ribbon right side out. Press the ribbon with the seam down the center, and overcast one end closed, tucking in the raw edge.

Whimsical alternatives to tabs are ribbon ties — ribbons of fabric that are sewed in pairs to the curtain top and tied around the rod in bows. The ribbons may match the fabric of the curtains, as shown above, or they can be made from a different cloth or in a different color.

To determine the fabric length for each ribbon, first allot 20 inches for the bow. Then add half of the rod's circumference, 1 inch to provide clearance between the rod and the curtain, and 1 inch to attach the ribbon to the curtain. To determine the total width of each ribbon, double its finished width — 1 inch is typical — and add ½ inch for a seam allowance.

Besides fabric, you will need a loop turner — a thin, 10-inch metal rod with a hooked end, designed to turn tubes of fabric inside out. Loop turners are inexpensive and are available wherever sewing supplies are sold.

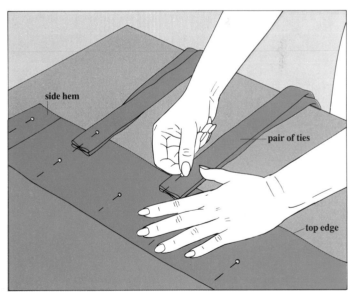

2 **Pinning on the ties.** Lay one ribbon atop another, seams together. Position the pair on the curtain and pin them with their unsewed ends 1 inch below the curtain top; the pinheads should be toward the top. Attach the lining and sew on the ties *(pages 58-59, Steps 7-8)*. Working with ribbons at one end of the curtain, tie a bow about 3 inches from the top edge. Slip the bow onto the rod and hang the curtain. Adjust the bow until the curtain is 1 inch off the floor; take down the curtain. Place a pin on each ribbon just below the knot. Measure and pin the same point on the remaining ribbons and use the pins as guides to make bows. Make final adjustments at the window.

A flourish of tent flaps

to which the board is fastened by screws, should not be more than ½ inch shorter than the board is wide.

To determine how long the mounting board should be, measure across the window frame from outside edge to outside edge and add the widths of two angle irons, plus 1 inch for a ½-inch overhang at each side.

To find the finished width of each curtain, start with half the length of the mounting board; add the width of the board for the return, plus 1½ inches for an overlap at the middle of the board. Then to determine the total width of fabric needed for one curtain, add 1 inch for two ½-inch side seam allowances.

A panel's finished length is the distance from wherever its bottom edge is to hang — here, 2½ inches below the window's apron — to the top of the front edge of the mounting board. Since the board is not mounted until after the curtain is completed, measure to the top of the window frame and add the board's thickness to determine the finished length. To find the total length of fabric necessary for a panel of that finished length, add the width of the mounting board and ½ inch for the bottom seam allowance. (The top of the curtain is left unseamed).

Cut the mounting board to size and cover it with fabric *(pages 108-109)* before starting the curtains. You can cover the board with standard white curtain lining material. But if instead you opt for the same fabric you are using for the lining of these curtains, the whole job will look that much better to anyone standing close enough to the window to see the bottom of the board.

The precise angles and smartly dressed lines of these easy-to-make curtains — known, for self-evident reasons, as tent flaps — impart a boldly sculpted form, especially when the curtains are done up, as here, in vivid primary colors for a child's room.

For tent-flap curtains, select heavy cotton, linen or canvas as face and lining fabrics. Light fabrics, such as silk or rayon, do not have enough body to hold the crisp, angular shapes that distinguish this window treatment. The color of the lining — always on show because the flaps are permanently open — can be in bold contrast to that of the face fabric, as it is here. Or you can choose related colors for a more subdued visual effect.

The curtains hang from a board mounted just above the window frame. This mounting board should be of sufficient width — the front-to-back measurement — that a plumb line dropped from its front edge would clear by 2 inches any blinds or shade on the window. The board is supported by angle irons fixed to the wall next to the side edges of the window frame; the angle irons' horizontal arms,

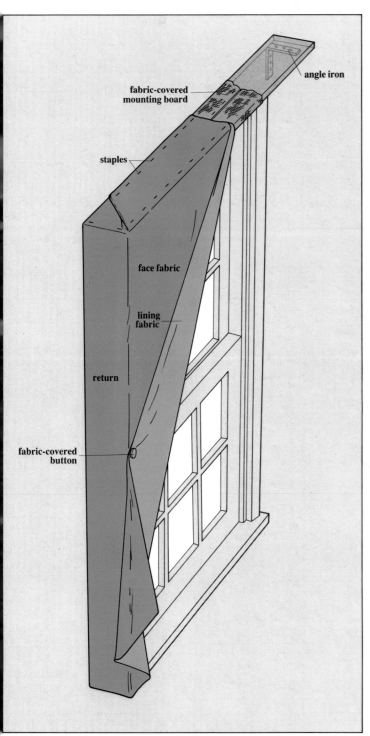

angle iron

fabric-covered
mounting board

staples

face fabric

lining
fabric

return

fabric-covered
button

A neat and simple panel. Each panel of a pair of tent-flap curtains consists of two layers of material: a face fabric and an equally attractive lining, which is on permanent display as the visible side of the turned-back flap. The face fabric and lining are sewed right sides together so the seams are hidden within the rectangular panel when it is turned right side out. The top portion of the panel — stapled to a fabric-clad mounting board supported by angle irons — is folded into a neatly mitered corner on the board's top, making the curtain's front and return hang straight in a boxlike form. The fabric-covered button is purely decorative; the flap is actually held in place by a concealed safety pin or tacking stitches.

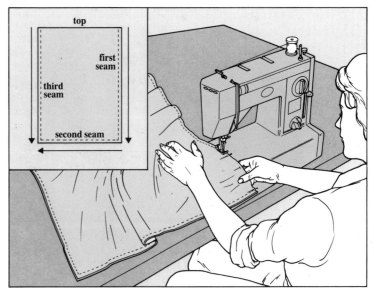

top

first
seam

third
seam

second seam

1 **Sewing the panels.** Cut the face fabric for each curtain to the required dimensions *(text, opposite)*, then use the pieces as patterns to cut the lining. Pin the face fabric to the lining, right sides together, with the pins perpendicular to the edges. Removing pins as you go, sew a straight seam ½ inch from the edge down one side of the panel, pivot and sew across the bottom *(inset, first and second seams)*. Turn the panel over and sew the third seam *(inset)* in the same direction as the first (sewing in the opposite direction might distort the fabric). At the end of the third seam, pivot and stitch an inch across the bottom before tying off the thread. Trim the seam allowances across the corners and clip any selvages every 3 to 4 inches. Turn each panel right side out and pull out the bottom corners with the tip of a pin *(page 68, Step 3)*. Finally, press the panels.

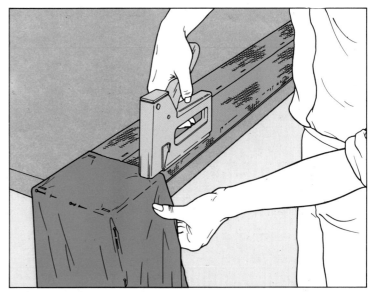

2 **Positioning a panel on the mounting board.** From several points along the bottom edge of each panel, measure toward the top the finished length of the curtain — the length to the upper front edge of the mounting board — and mark that line across the curtain with pins. Then place the left-hand panel's top left corner, face fabric up, over the left end of the covered mounting board: Align the panel's left edge with the back of the mounting board and the finished-length pins with the upper side edge of the board. Staple the panel to the top of the board at four places. ▶

3 **Fastening the rest of the panel.** Bring the top of the free portion of the panel around the front of the mounting board so that the finished-length pins lie along the top of the board's front edge. Fold under the left-hand end of this portion of fabric along a diagonal line to form a mitered corner *(right)*. Staple the fabric to the top of the board at 3-inch intervals along the board's front and back edges, and remove all the pins.

　　Now repeat Steps 2 and 3 to attach the right-hand curtain to the mounting board, overlapping the left-hand curtain at the middle of the board by 1½ inches.

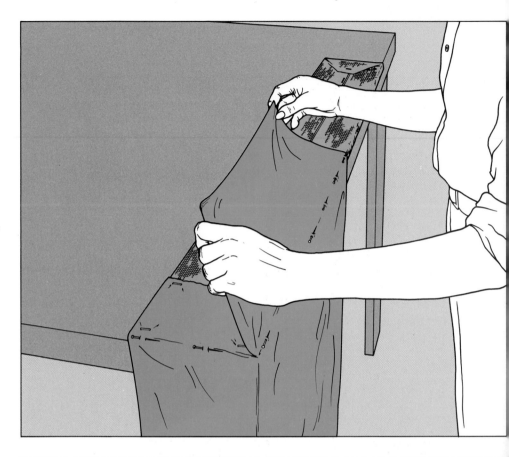

4 **Positioning the mounting board.** Determine what kind of fasteners you will need *(pages 124-125)* to attach to the wall the angle irons that will support the mounting board. Fix the angle irons in place on the wall against the outside edges of the window frame, their top surfaces flush with the top of the frame.

　　Drape the curtains out of the way over the ends of the mounting board, and set the board on top of the frame and the angle irons. While a helper holds the board, measure to make sure its ends extend the same distance beyond the angle irons on both sides of the window. Then fix the board to the angle irons with flat-head screws of a diameter to fit the angle-iron holes and short enough so they penetrate only partway through the board. Spread the curtains so that they hang straight.

Covering a Button

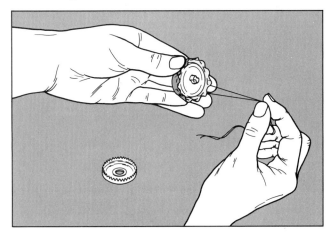

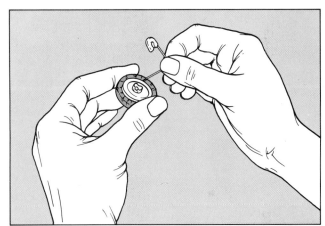

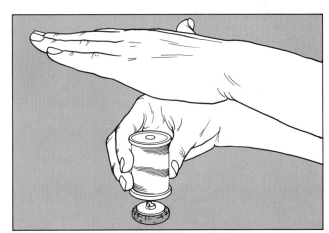

5 **Turning back the flap.** From the top of each front corner of the mounting board, measure halfway down the length of the panel. Mark that place with a pin on the front of the curtain, next to where the fabric rounds the corner to form the return. Fold back each panel as shown above until its leading edge just covers the pin, and mark that place on the lining fabric of the turned-back flap with another pin. Now cover two buttons with lining fabric (*right*) and sew them onto the flaps at the pin-marked places. Then secure each flap in its open position, either by tacking it to the curtain's face with several stitches behind the button, or by pinning it there with a safety pin.

Button shells designed for covering are available in several sizes wherever fabrics are sold. To use the type shown here, first cut a circle of fabric 1 inch larger in diameter than the shell. Sew short basting stitches ⅛ inch from the edge of the material, leaving loose 4-inch-long thread ends. Then pull the ends of the thread to form a pouch. Insert the shell and tighten the thread (*top*). Set the button's metal back over the shank of the shell, but do not push it all the way down. Use a safety pin to tuck the fabric snugly beneath the teeth of the button back (*middle*). Secure the metal back by slipping a spool's hole over the shank and pushing on the spool (*bottom*).

Stately swags and jabots

The casual elegance of a long curtain tossed back over its rod to admit light has evolved into stylized swags and jabots, or cascades. Unlike many window treatments, swags and jabots require minimal sewing. They derive their form from precise measuring and diligent folding, pinning and pressing at every stage of the process.

The decorative effect of swags and jabots will vary with the fabric chosen. The striped cotton shown at left, for example, produces a crisp, tailored drapery, whereas a damask would underscore the luxuriousness of the multiple pleats. The fabric always should be rich, of medium or heavy weight, and soft: A stiff fabric will not fall into attractive folds. Because the lining will be visible in the jabot pleats, it must be of a coordinated high-quality fabric.

Most curtain fabrics are 48 or 54 inches wide — ample for the standard swag and jabot patterns in Step 1, which are designed for conventional windows 36 to 48 inches wide and at least 56 inches tall.

For a broader window, a more natural look is achieved by hanging two or three overlapping swags of the size shown here rather than by constructing one wide swag. The jabot pattern may be cut as much as 6 inches shorter across the top to fit a smaller window, but its shortest pleat should hang lower than the swag, which measures 15 inches at its center when completed.

For other window sizes, use the proportions of these patterns as guides to make your own patterns with trial, error and kraft paper.

At the window shown, the mounting board holding the drapery in place is a nominal 1-by-6 — a standard board actually measuring ¾ inch by 5½ inches — that has been painted and is screwed directly into the frame. Alternatively, the board could be wrapped in fabric *(pages 108-109, Steps 10-11);* it could also be fastened inside or outside the frame with angle irons *(page 100).*

If your window frame is shallower than 6 inches, use a 1-by-4 board for an inside mount and subtract 2 inches from both the width and length of the jabot pattern at its longer side.

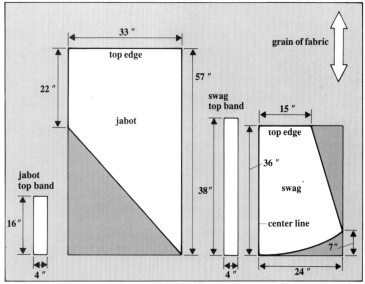

1 **Swag and jabot patterns.** Cut patterns from kraft paper or muslin in the dimensions shown above, drawing the curved bottom of the swag free-hand. Then cut out two jabot front panels and two lining panels for each window. The two jabots mirror each other; cut one jabot panel, then turn the pattern over to cut the second panel from the area of fabric print that provides the best match. Cut two lining panels the same way. To cut the swag, fold the fabric down the middle lengthwise, and press lightly. Place the pattern's center line along the fold, pin the pattern to the fabric and cut through both thicknesses. Cut the swag lining the same way. The top bands may be cut from fabric scraps.

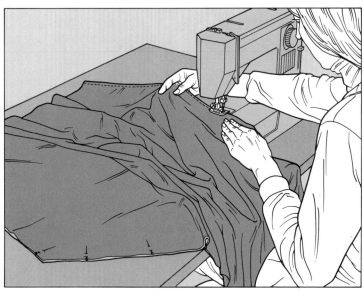

2 **Sewing the jabot lining to the front.** Align one front jabot panel to one jabot lining panel, placing them face to face and pinning them together along the edges. Sew along the sides and bottom, leaving a ½-inch seam allowance. Do not sew the top edge. Remove the pins. ▶

A mounting board for simple installation. Bands of fabric sewed across the tops of the swag and jabots are stapled to a 1-by-6 cut to fit inside the window frame. The board has been painted to match the window frame, thus camouflaging its presence. After the swag and jabots are attached, the mounting board is fastened to the top jamb of the frame with screws (Step 13). Here, the jabots overlap the swag to emphasize the stripes in the fabric. However, the swag may drape over the jabots instead for a softer, richer look.

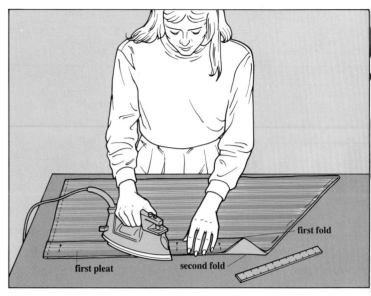

3 **Finishing the jabot panel.** Turn the front panel and the lining right side out. Pull the seams straight and pick out the corners fully with a pin *(above)*. Spread the panel flat, front side down, and press the edges flat. Pin the front and lining together along the top edge and sew that edge closed, leaving a ½-inch seam allowance.

4 **Folding the first pleat.** Lay the jabot panel flat, face upward, with the short side away from you. Turn the short side under, forming a fold 3 inches from the panel edge, and press. Double the fold back over the face of the panel, forming a second fold 3 inches from the first fold and even with the panel edge. These two folds form the first pleat, shown above. Press the pleat well and pin it in place.

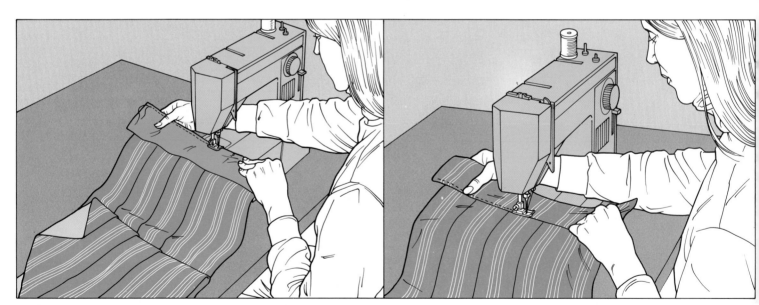

6 **Attaching the jabot top band.** Align the top band along the top edge of the jabot, face to face, and pin it in place. Stitch the two pieces together ½ inch from the edge *(above, left)*. Remove the pins and turn the band face upward. Topstitch the top band ¼ inch from the first row of stitches *(above, right)* to reinforce the seam between the two pieces. Repeat Steps 2-6 to make the other jabot.

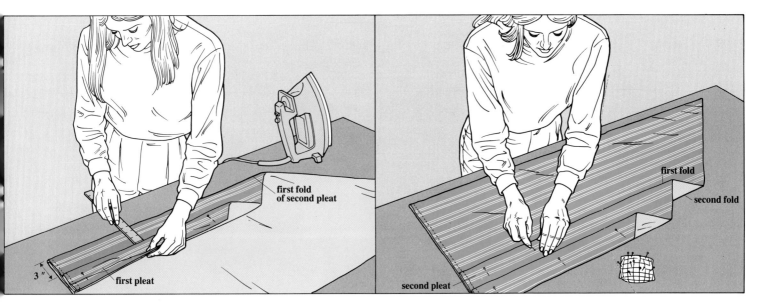

first fold
of second pleat

first pleat

first fold

second fold

second pleat

3"

5 **Forming the second pleat.** Turn the panel face downward, the pleat toward you. Fold the pleated edge back over the lining *(above, left)* so that the first fold of the first pleat is 3 inches from the edge of the new fold; then press and pin this fold. Flip the panel face upward, the pleated edge away from you, and double the fold back over the panel face toward you *(above, right),* forming the second fold of the second pleat 3 inches from the first fold and even with the first fold of the first pleat. Press and pin the second pleat. Repeat this step to form the third pleat. Baste the pleats in place across the top, ½ inch from the edge.

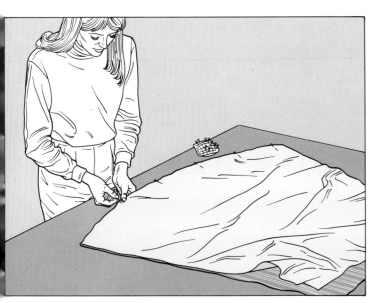

7 **Pinning together the swag front and lining.** Lay the swag front face up and spread the lining over it face down, their curved edges aligned. Pin the panels together at 6-inch intervals along the curve, adding a few extra pins up the side edges for stability. Stitch along the curved edge only, leaving a ½-inch seam allowance, and remove the pins.

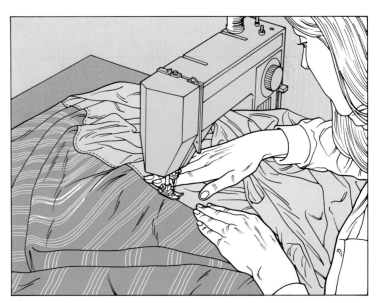

8 **Topstitching the curved edge of the swag.** Spread out the swag front and lining so that both are face upward and the seam allowance is beneath the lining. Stitch a seam through the seam allowance along the curved edge of the lining, ¼ inch from the first seam *(above).* Press the lining panel to the back of the front panel along the curved edge. Pin the swag front and lining together at the remaining three sides and sew them with a ½-inch seam allowance. Remove the pins. ▶

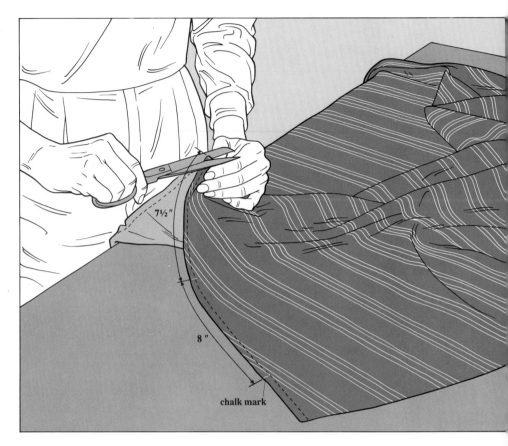

9 **Cutting pleat-position notches.** With chalk, mark notch positions on the seam allowance along each side edge of the swag panel, measuring down from the top corners at intervals of 5½ inches, 7 inches, 7½ inches and 8 inches. At each mark, pinch a fold in the swag edge and cut off a tiny triangle of fabric, taking care not to cut into the seam.

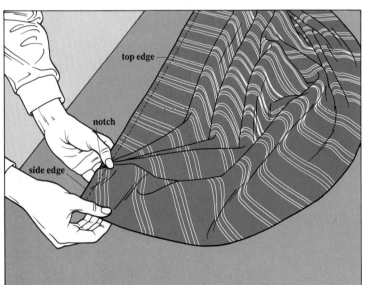

11 **Gathering the final pleats.** When bringing the last notch at each side to the top corner, turn the side edge of the swag parallel to the top edge before pinning (above). Lift the swag to check its drape, and adjust the pin positions very slightly if necessary. Baste the pleats in place ½ inch from the top edge of the swag. Remove the pins and apply the top band as for the jabots (Step 6).

12 **Stapling the swag to the mounting board.** Center the swag top band along the mounting board, its stitched edge ⅛ inch in from the board's edge so that the band will not show when hung. Staple the band to the board at one end, then stretch it smooth and staple the other end. Staple between the two ends at 6-inch intervals.

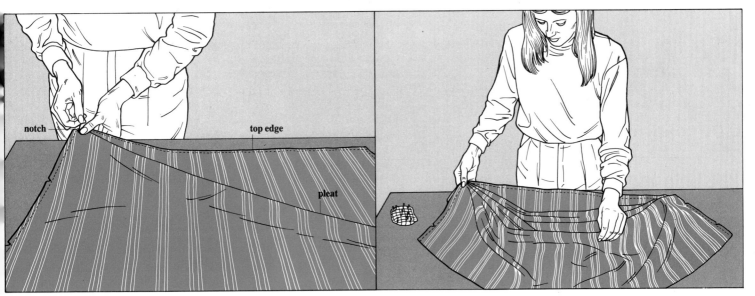

10 **Pleating the swag.** Lay the swag panel face up, its top edge toward you. Pinch the first notch on one side between your fingers, pull it to the top corner and pin it in place *(above, left)*. Pin the first notch on the other side to the opposite corner. Continue pinning notches to the corners, alternating sides and keeping the top edge perfectly straight. Lift the swag by the corners and shake it gently *(above, right)* to encourage the gathers to fall symmetrically.

13 **Attaching the jabots.** Place the top band of one jabot at the end of the mounting board, with the jabot's shortest pleat overlapping the swag and its longest pleat even with the corner of the board. Staple the band in place. Position the mounting board with its end, and the jabot, hanging over the table's edge. Wrap the long edge of the jabot around the end of the board, tucking in excess top-band fabric, and staple the band in place *(right)*. Attach the second jabot at the opposite end the same way. Install the mounting board against the top jamb of the window frame with 2-inch No. 12 wood screws, 6 inches from each end.

Pinch pleats in the formal tradition

Evenly spaced pinch pleats — three or four folds of heading pinched tightly together — are the traditional finish for many formal curtains, especially draw draperies hung on traverse rods. Pleating creates controlled fullness in fabric: When the curtains are closed, pleats spaced at regular intervals ensure that the fabric's fullness is evenly distributed across the window. When the curtains are pulled open, pleats gather the fabric into straight, regimented folds.

Pleats can be made in various styles (pages 77-78), but the three-fold pinch pleat shown on both the opaque draperies and the sheer curtains below is by far the most popular. The actual shaping of pinch pleats is not difficult. The tricky part of the process is figuring out the curtain yardage and plotting the position of the pleats.

To determine the width of fabric you will need for a pair of full-length pleated curtains that will draw across a window, measure the installed traverse rod from corner to corner and multiply by three. Add twice the rod return, plus the number of inches the two master slides will overlap when pulled together at the center. For length, measure from the top of the rod to the floor, subtract ½ inch for clearance, then add 12 inches for a 4-inch double hem at the floor and a 4-inch single hem at the heading.

Make a pair of floor-length panels of the requisite width, using the technique shown for the tab curtains on pages 56-60. Cut lining for the panels 7 inches shorter than the unfinished length of the face fabric, and machine-stitch a 2-inch double hem at the bottom. Press in a 4-inch single top hem. Place each lining panel, seamed side down, on the back of the curtain-fabric panel; finger-press 1½-inch hems down each side, using a hemming gauge as a guide. Then pin the lining to the face fabric at the top and sides, ¼ inch from the top, and plot the pleats as explained opposite.

The small folds that constitute each pleat are tacked together with a needle and thread. You will need a thimble to push the needle through all of the folds, which are made up of 12 layers of curtain fabric, 12 additional layers of lining and six layers of buckram. Use a size 7 sharp dressmaking needle and a china thimble. Do not use a metal thimble: The pressure that is required to push the needle

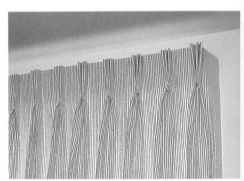

through all of the layers can cause the top of the needle to puncture the metal.

Once the curtains are completed, they should be hung immediately to prevent unnecessary wrinkling. They must then be trained to hang in even folds, a process that first involves what is known as "breaking" the heading. The buckram-lined fabric space between each pair of pleats is pulled forward into sharp folds. The fabric — like an accordion — will compress into these folds when the curtain is drawn open. Next, the fabric is tied together for two or three days. This sets the folds and helps press out wrinkles. After they are untied, the curtains should be opened and closed frequently for the following several days to shake out any remaining wrinkles.

Plotting pleats. Figure out the size and location of pleats after making the curtain panel and pinning the lining to it. The example below is a diagram of a panel put together according to the directions in the text at left. Some artistic liberties have been taken for the sake of clarity: The size of the pins is exaggerated and only marking pins — no fastening pins — are shown in the heading.

Start your pleat calculations by estimating the number of pleats and spaces. As a rule, count on five pleats per width of fabric and two pleats for every half width. One less space than pleats is needed. Thus, for a two-width panel, you would estimate 10 pleats and nine spaces.

For one of a pair of draw draperies, subtract the finished width of one curtain (half the length of the rod, plus one return and the overlap) from the width of the panel. The result is the overall pleat allowance (the amount of material that will be drawn into pleats). Divide the overall pleat allowance by the number of pleats to get the individual pleat allowance — the amount of fabric that will be taken up by each pleat.

Next, divide half of the length of the rod from corner to corner by the number of spaces. The result is the space allowance — the amount of space between each pair of pleats.

For three-fold pinch pleats, allow 5½ to 7½ inches for each pleat and 4 to 5 inches for each space. If your results do not fall within this range, try the calculations again, revising your original estimates. If either the pleat allowance or the space allowance is greater than it should be, add a pleat and a space; if the allowances measure less than they should,

subtract a pleat and a space.

Transfer the final measurements to the curtain, marking with pins. Mark off the return, then starting with a pleat, mark alternating pleat and space allowances across the heading. Check to see that the panel is divided so that any seams fall in or next to a pleat allowance; the seams will then be concealed by the folds of the finished pleats. If a seam falls in a space allowance, rearrange the pins. In this case, there may be slight variations in the pleat allowances; these will be barely noticeable on the finished curtains. However, size differences are more obvious with spaces, so keep all spaces an equal width.

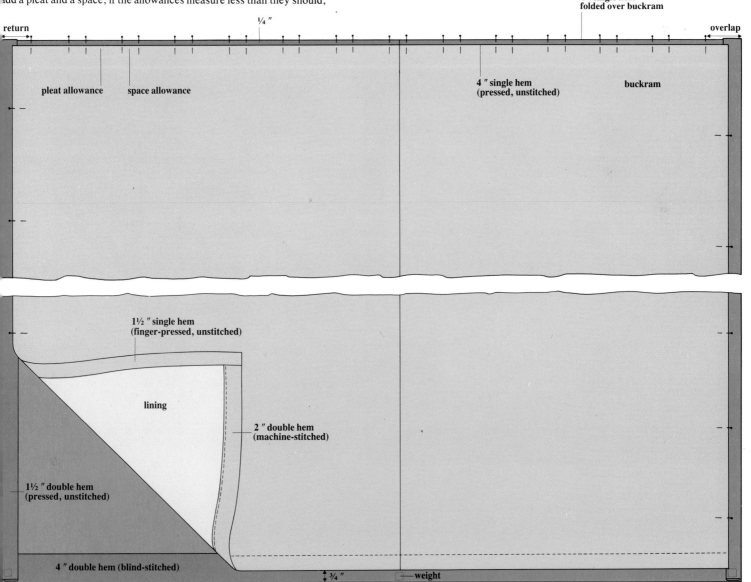

1 **Pinning the pleats.** Working from the back of the panel, fold the heading — including the lining — into deep single pleats by bringing together adjacent marking pins in pairs. Firmly finger-press each fold as you proceed and pin the pleats together where the marking pins meet. After creasing and pinning all of the pleats, measure across the top of the heading to check that it equals the finished width of the curtain panel — one half the length of the rod, plus the return and the overlap. Adjust the size of the pleats if the measurements do not match.

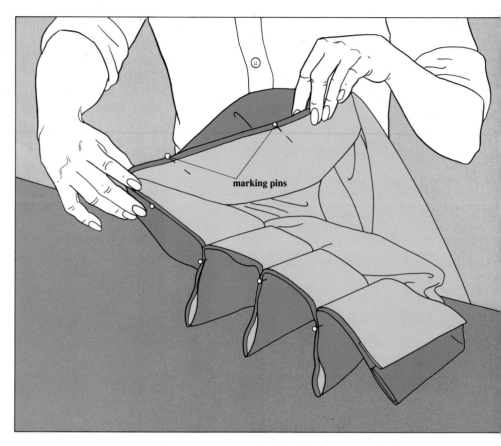

marking pins

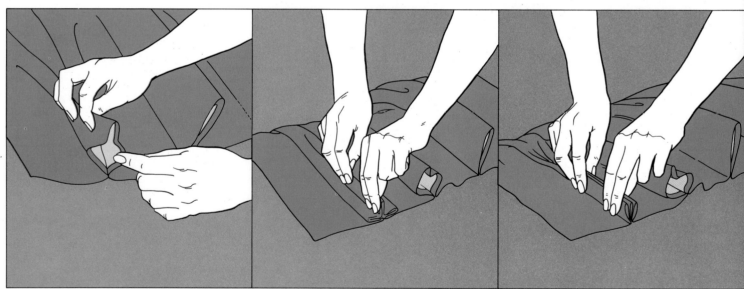

4 **Forming a pinch pleat.** Turn the curtain right side up and lay it on a firm surface. Have a china thimble and a needle threaded with a double unknotted thread ready. With one hand, pinch the fold of a pleat a couple of inches below the top of the heading while using the other hand to open up the top of the pleat *(above, left)*. Next, with both hands, press the fold straight down to meet the seam beneath it; the extra fabric will bend out to both sides, forming two additional folds *(above, center)*. Now pinch the two outside folds up to meet the center fold and lightly finger-crease the three folds together *(above, right)*, checking to see that they are of equal size.

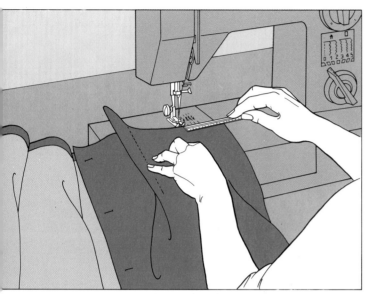

2 **Sewing the pleats.** Set the sewing machine's stitch-length dial to seven stitches to the inch. Working on the front of the curtain, use a hemming gauge, set at the exact depth of the pleat minus the width of the presser foot, as a guide to stitch each pleat parallel to the crease. Sew from the top of the panel to the bottom of the buckram stiffener. Lock-stitch at each end of the seam.

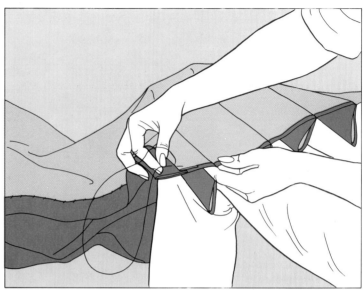

3 **Fastening the lining.** Turn the curtain over, and blind-stitch the lining to the curtain fabric up one side and across the top of the panel to the first pleat *(above)*. Remove pins as you go. Then blind-stitch the other side. Leave the bottom of the lining loose. At the top, the lining is secured by being incorporated into the pleats.

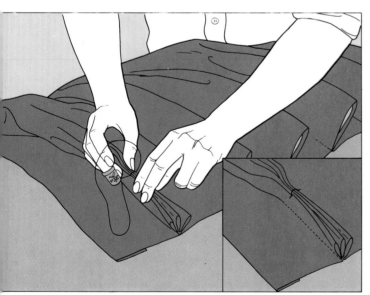

5 **Tacking the pleat.** At the base of the pleat (a little less than 4 inches from the top), push the threaded needle through all the layers of fabric and buckram. Pull the thread through, leaving a ⅛-inch tail. Loop the thread back over the folds and push the needle through twice more, pulling it taut each time. Snip the thread off close to the pleat *(inset).* ▶

Pleater Tape

With narrow vertical pockets spaced at regular intervals, buckram pleater tape 3 to 4 inches wide is a speedy alternative to hand-sewing pleats. The tape is machine-stitched directly to the top of lined or unlined curtain panels made without buckram stiffening in the heading. The three-fold pleats are formed by inserting special four-pronged pleater hooks into the pockets.

The size of the curtain panel is determined by the tape. Before cutting the fabric, use the hooks to prepleat the tape to the curtain's desired finished width, and hang the tape on the rod. Leave enough unpleated space for the return and, at the opposite end, for the overlap. Use a single pocket at each end for single end hooks. With a pencil, lightly mark all of the pockets containing hooks and remove the hooks. The stretched-out tape is the width for the curtain panel.

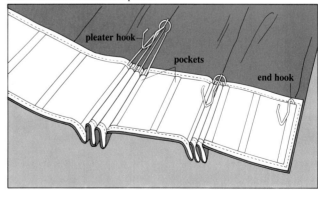

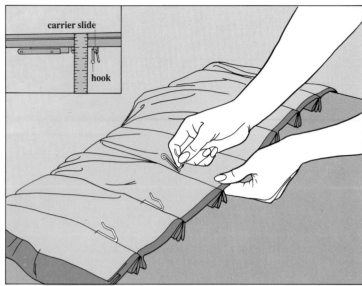

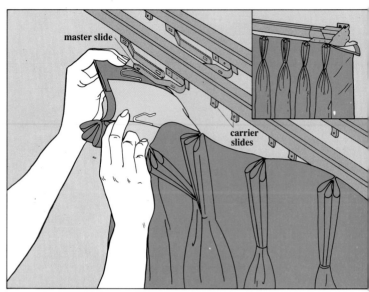

6 **Putting in the hooks.** To determine the position of the drapery hooks in the heading, first hang a hook from one of the carrier slides on the traverse rod. Measure from the top edge of the rod to the bottom of the hook *(inset).* Measure the same distance from the top of the heading down the back of each pleat, then lightly mark that point with a pencil. Stick the pointed end of a drapery hook into each seam at the mark and push the hook up into the seam. At the return side of the panel, place a hook on the edge; at the overlap side, put a hook ½ inch in from the edge.

7 **Hanging the curtains.** Have a helper hold the curtain while you hook it to the rod. (A double rod is shown here.) Begin at the master slide. Put the first hook in the first hole in the slide and the second hook in the next-closest hole. You may have to adjust the position of the first hook so that the space between the two hooks more closely matches the space between the holes. Put hooks in each successive carrier slide, pushing the extras to the end of the rod. Remove superfluous slides — or add extras, if needed — by slipping them through the end gate *(page 28).* Hook the return end of the curtain to the bracket *(inset).*

8 **Training the curtains.** Start by "breaking" the heading: Place your finger behind the space between two pleats, pull that section of heading forward and crease it lightly in the center *(inset).* Repeat for all of the spaces. Next, open the curtains to their full, stacked-back position. Use your fingers as a comb to form neat folds from the heading down to the floor. Finally, tie the folds in place with soft cord or ribbon. Leave the curtains tied for two or three days to set the folds.

Pleating Sheer Fabrics

Sheer curtains hung as undertreatments on the inside rod of a pair of traverse rods are ½ inch shorter than their opaque counterparts, but they are made in almost exactly the same way. The curtain panels are unlined, with a 4-inch double hem at the bottom and 1½-inch double hems at the sides. At the heading, a 4-inch double hem is folded over the buckram *(right)* so that the cut edges of the fabric do not show through from the front of the panel. The pinch pleats are plotted in the same way as those on page 73. There is no return on the inner rod of a double traverse rod, so you should place the first pleat near the outside edge of the panel, about 3 inches in from the edge.

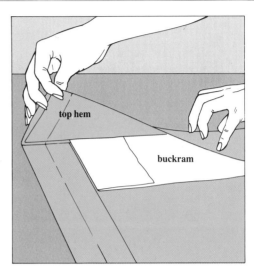

Four-Fold Pleats

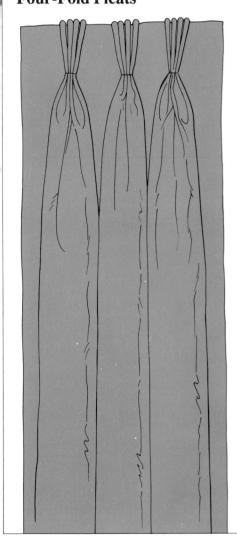

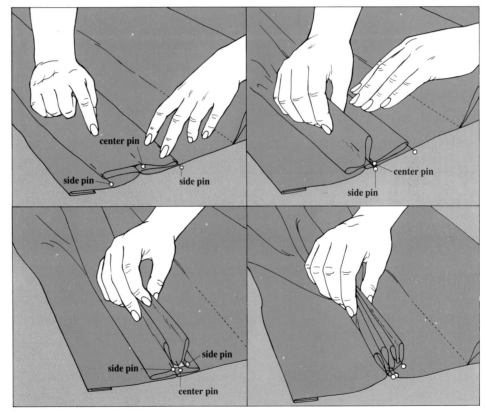

The four-fold pinch pleat looks like the three-fold pinch pleat but uses more fabric and yields fuller folds. Following the pleat-plotting method shown on page 73, allow 7 to 9 inches for each pleat and 4 to 5 inches for the spaces between them. After stitching the pleat allowances and attaching the curtain lining *(page 75, Steps 2-3)*, mark the center of each fold with a pin.

Flatten the pleat so that the pin aligns with the pleat-allowance seam, then mark the side creases with pins *(top left)*. Invert one of the side creases by aligning the side pin with the center pin *(top right);* similarly, align the side pin on the opposite side with the center pin *(bottom left)*. Pinch the folds together at the base of the heading *(bottom right)*, then tack them as in Step 5, page 75.

Cartridge Pleats

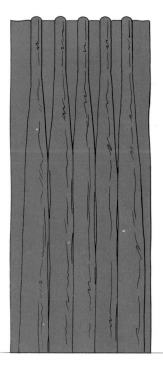

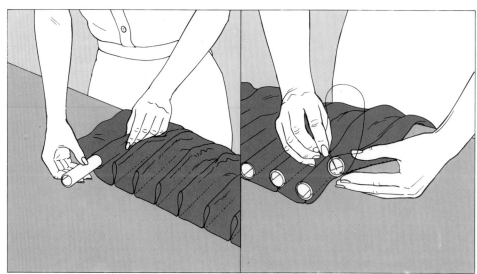

Cartridge pleats produce curtains with narrow, columnar folds. They suit sheer curtains as well as opaque ones made of lightweight fabric. Cartridge pleats require a 3- to 4-inch pleat allowance and a 3- to 4-inch space allowance *(page 73)*. Stitch the pleats *(page 75, Step 2)* without creasing them.

Then, for each pleat, cut a piece of 4-inch buckram 10 inches long and roll it crosswise into a tight cylinder. Slip the cylinder into the pleat *(above, left)*; it will spring open to fill the space snugly. Secure each pleat by tacking the cylinder to the heading on both sides of the pleat-allowance seam *(above, right)*.

Box Pleats

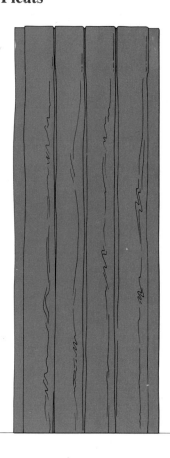

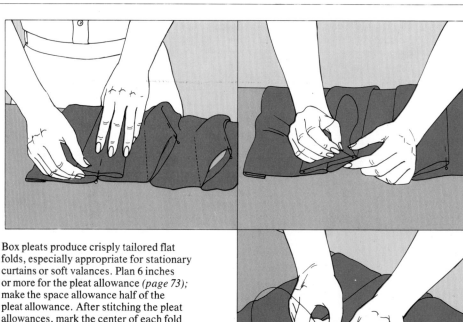

Box pleats produce crisply tailored flat folds, especially appropriate for stationary curtains or soft valances. Plan 6 inches or more for the pleat allowance *(page 73)*; make the space allowance half of the pleat allowance. After stitching the pleat allowances, mark the center of each fold with a pin. Flatten the pleat, aligning the pin with the pleat-allowance seam *(above, left)*. Then — removing pins as you go — secure each side of the pleat with several tacking stitches about 1/16 inch below the top of the heading *(above, right)*. Finally, to make the pleat lie flat, take several fastening stitches through the back and inner layer about 1/4 inch above the base of the heading and 1/4 inch in from the side crease *(right)*.

Tiebacks: The finishing touch

Curtain tiebacks may seem minor characters in the cast of a full window treatment, but their role is important. By holding the curtains back from the window in graceful curves, tiebacks add beauty to a room while opening it to light and air.

Tiebacks can take many forms, including decorative ropes or chains. And metal holdbacks *(photograph, page 44)* can secure narrow curtains. Tiebacks made of fabric, like those at right, are the most popular devices, however.

Fabric tiebacks can be made with straight, parallel edges. But contoured tiebacks like the top two at right, with a curved bottom edge that is longer than the top edge, allow curtains to fan out gently below. Instructions for making basic contoured tiebacks are on the following two pages. The addition of welting — a fabric-covered cotton cord sewed into the tieback's seam *(middle right)* — can give the tieback a professionally tailored appearance. Instructions for welted tiebacks on pages 82-83 include directions for making welting. The fabric for welting is cut on the bias — diagonally to the grain *(page 82, Step 1)* — so it will be flexible enough to bend smoothly around corners.

A ruffled curtain is best matched with a ruffled tieback *(bottom right)*; the tieback ruffle should be the same width as the curtain ruffle. Instructions for making ruffled tiebacks are on pages 84-85.

Reinforcing tiebacks with interfacing helps them retain their shape under the weight of the curtains. A fusible, nonwoven interfacing is used for the projects that follow; it bonds to the fabric in seconds when pressed with a steam iron.

A ⅜-inch bone or brass ring is sewed to each end of a tieback; plastic rings might break in dry cleaning. The rings are then secured to a hooked fastener *(page 81, Step 5)* or to a tieback support *(page 86)* that holds the curtains out from the wall. (When a support is used, the tieback pattern's dimensions are calculated differently: See page 86.) The hook or support is hidden just inside the curtain's outer edge. Some professional installers recommend that the tiebacks encircle the curtains 42 inches above the floor; others suggest they be at window-sill height. The best advice is to position them wherever they are most agreeable to your eye. Always install the tieback hooks or supports before starting work on the tiebacks.

The Basic Contoured Form

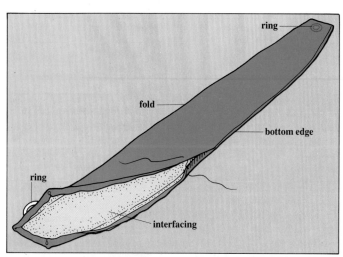

A simple fold of fabric. This tieback is constructed from a single piece of fabric fused to a layer of interfacing and folded lengthwise. The fabric is cut to form a gentle curve along the tieback's bottom edge, so that the tieback is narrower at the ends than in the middle. A hidden seam — mainly stitched by machine — closes the tieback's ends and bottom. Rings sewed to the ends secure the tieback to a hook beside the window.

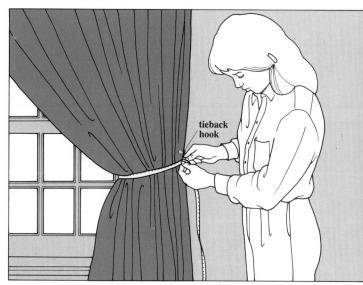

1 **Measuring for tiebacks.** Hold one end of a cloth tape measure against the tieback hook secured in the wall. Bring the tape around the curtain and back to the hook. Adjust the tape and the curtain until you like the tied-back effect; the measurement on the tape is the finished length for each tieback. To figure the length to cut, add a 1-inch seam allowance. To determine the finished width, fold a piece of fabric lengthwise and hold it around the curtain, adjusting the fold until you find a pleasing width. The tiebacks shown on page 79 are 3½ inches wide. Cut fabric double the finished width and add a 1-inch seam allowance.

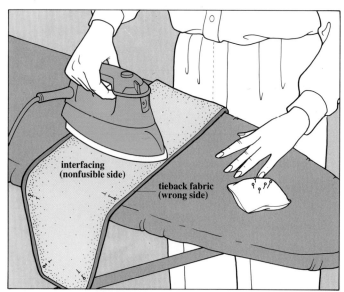

3 **Fusing the interfacing.** Use the pattern to cut two tiebacks from the face fabric and two pieces of fusible interfacing. Pin a piece of interfacing, fusible side down, to the wrong side of each piece of tieback fabric. With scissors, trim away ¼ inch from the edges of the interfacing. Fuse the interfacing to the fabric with a steam iron set for a permanent-press fabric, pressing the iron firmly on each section of interfacing for 10 seconds and removing the pins as you proceed. Overlap each ironed section slightly to ensure a good bond.

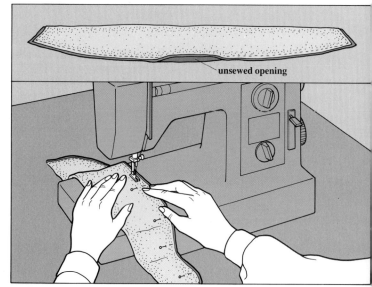

4 **Stitching the tieback.** Fold each tieback lengthwise, right sides facing, and pin the cut edges together. Beginning at one end, lock-stitch and sew a seam ½ inch from the tieback's edge. When you reach the midpoint of the edge, stop, raise the needle and presser foot, and move the tieback along to leave an opening of about 4 inches (inset). Then lower the presser foot and continue the seam, lock-stitching at the end. Clip the thread at the seam's opening. Turn the tieback right side out and iron it, pressing in the seam allowances along the opening. Use small overcast hand stitches to sew the opening closed.

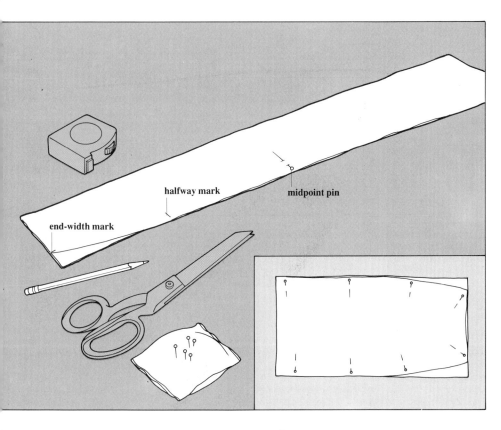

2 Cutting a pattern. Cut a piece of scrap fabric or kraft paper to the dimensions established in Step 1. Fold it in half lengthwise, press it with an iron, and pin the cut edges together. Bring the strip's ends together just long enough to mark its midpoint with a pin.

Make a pencil mark on the cut edge halfway between the midpoint pin and one end of the strip. Along that end, measure down from the fold a width 1½ inches narrower than the finished width of the tieback; however, this measured width should not be less than 2 inches. Add a ½-inch seam allowance and mark that point with a pencil.

Draw a curving line connecting the pencil mark on the end with the pencil mark on the long cut edge. Cut the curve with scissors. Unpin and open the strip, fold it in half crosswise, and pin together the ends and then the sides *(inset)*. Trim the uncut end to match the curved end.

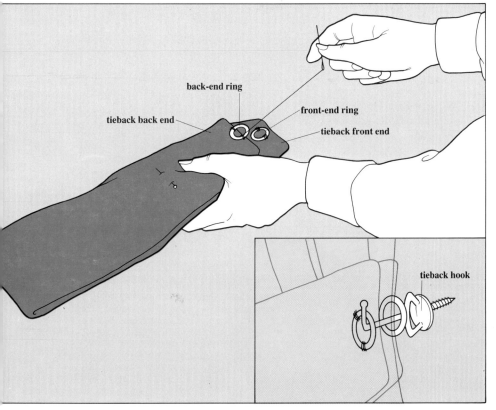

5 Sewing on the rings. Designate one tieback for the left-hand side of the window and one for the right-hand side. Lay each one flat and fold it crosswise so the end that will be behind the curtain falls about an inch short of the end that will be in front of the curtain, as seen at left. Pin the front and rear sections together to keep their side edges aligned.

Center a ⅜-inch ring on the rear side of the tieback's front section, ¼ inch from the end. Sew it in place with loop stitches *(page 42, Step 8)* that only pierce the first layer of fabric. Then sew another ring to the rear section, in line with the first ring and extending about ¼ inch beyond the tieback's end, as shown.

Unpin the tieback. Slip its back-end ring over the hook, wrap the tieback around the curtain, and secure the front-end ring *(inset)*.

Adding Tailored Welting

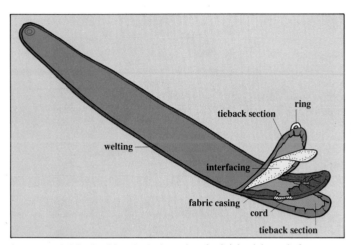

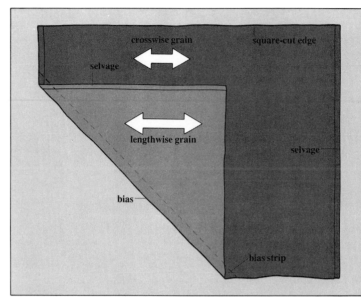

A contoured tieback with welted edges. A welted tieback is made from two sections of fabric, one of them bonded to a layer of fusible interfacing. The welting is a ¼-inch cord sewed into a fabric casing. The same stitches that hold the two sides of the tieback together also pass through the welting's seam allowances where they are sandwiched inside the tieback, and thus hold the welting in place along the tieback's edges.

1 **Preparing for the welting.** Following instructions on pages 80-81, cut fabric for two contoured tiebacks and interfacing for one. Fold and cut each of these pieces in half lengthwise, fuse interfacing to two of the fabric sections, then set them all aside. Now fold a squared piece of fabric (*above*) so a selvage is in line with a square-cut edge and the lengthwise grain of the folded corner is parallel to the crosswise grain of the remaining fabric. Cut off the corner along the diagonal fold. Now cut a 2-inch-wide strip (*dotted line*) on the bias — parallel to the diagonal edge.

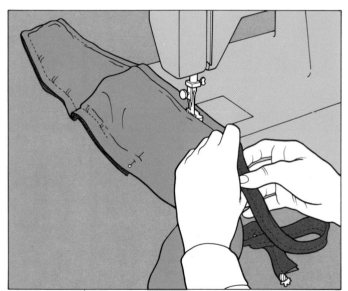

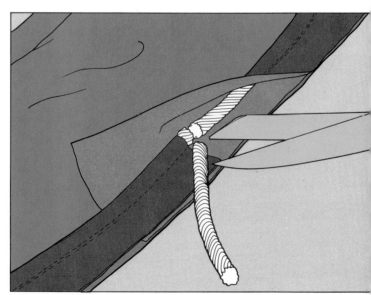

4 **Sewing on the welting.** Lay a tieback section without interfacing right side up. Pin one end of the welting to the middle of one long side of the tieback section — the cord edge of the welting on the inside and the welting's cut edges aligned with the tieback's cut edge. Turn the tieback wrong side up, keeping its edges aligned with the welting's edges. Using the zipper presser foot, start stitching 2 inches from the pin, close to the cord but not crowding it. Sew around the tieback's perimeter, curving the welting at the ends. Stop stitching 2 inches from the end of the welting.

5 **Clipping the cord.** Remove the tieback from the machine. Turn it right side up. Fold back the 2 inches of open cord casing at one end of the welting to expose the end of the cord. Leaving at least ½ inch of welting free from the tieback on each end, trim both the exposed and fabric-covered cord ends until they just fit together, end to end.

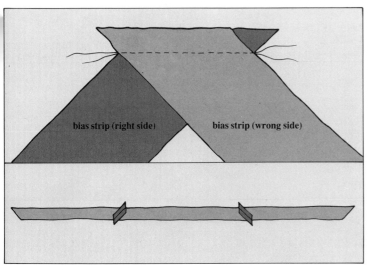

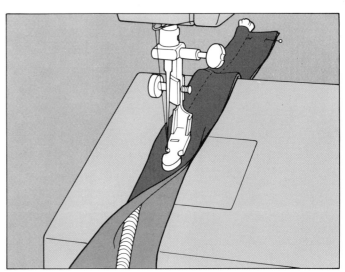

2 **Joining bias strips.** Measure the perimeter of a tieback section and add 3 inches to determine the length of ¼-inch-diameter cord and the length of fabric to cover it that you will need for the welting. If the bias strip cut in Step 1 is not long enough to form the whole casing, cut additional 2-inch-wide strips on the bias — that is, parallel to the first diagonal cut. Allow an extra inch of length for each place where two strips will be seamed together. To create one long piece, pin the ends of the strips right sides together so they form a V, and stitch them ½ inch from the short edges *(top picture above)*. Then lay the joined strips out flat and press the seams open *(lower picture above)*.

3 **Stitching the welting.** Lay the welting fabric strip wrong side up and place a cord along its center line. Bring the cut edges of the strip together around the cord, and pin one end. Using a zipper press-er foot on the machine, sew a seam close alongside the cord without crowding against it. Stop stitching about 2 inches from the other end of the cord and lock your stitches. Then trim the excess fabric of the cord seam allowance to about ½ inch.

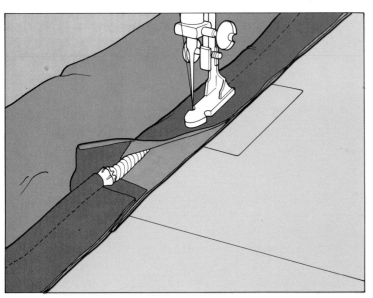

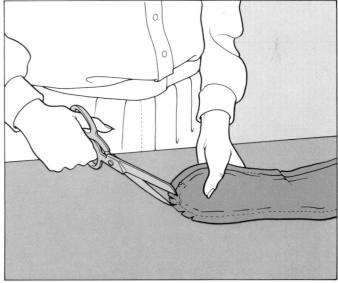

6 **Stitching the casing closed.** Fold under the end of the open cord casing, as seen above, and fit it around both ends of the cord to cover the point where they meet. Place the tieback, right side up, under the machine's presser foot at this point. Stitch the cord casing closed.

7 **Completing the tieback.** Pin a welted tieback section to an inter-faced section, right sides together. Place the tieback under the press-er foot, welted section on top. Lock-stitch and sew close to the cord. On one long side, raise the needle and presser foot, and pull the tieback through to leave a 4-inch opening; finish the seam, lock-stitching at the end. Trim the seam allowance to ¼ inch. At the tie-back's ends, clip from the edge down to the seam *(above)*. Turn the tieback right side out, press it lightly with an iron, and hand-stitch the opening closed. Sew rings to the ends *(page 81, Step 5)*.

A Ruffled Version

The ruffled tieback. This tieback is sewed from two pieces of fabric — one for the ruffle and one for the narrow band. Each piece is folded in half lengthwise. The ruffle's cut edges are held between the band's folded-under edges. A doubled piece of interfacing within the band keeps the band from crumpling under the weight of the curtains.

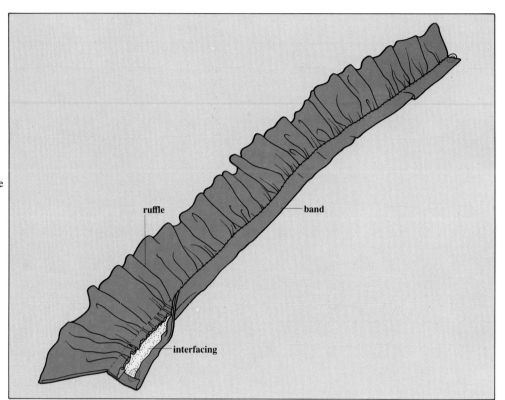

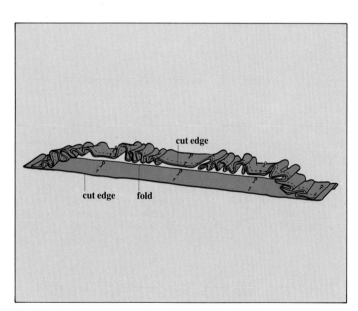

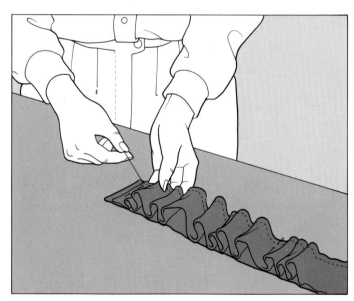

2 Pinning the ruffle to the band. Turn the band right side up and lay the ruffle strip atop the band, aligning its cut edges with the cut edge of the band. Pin the ends of the ruffle strip to the band, ½ inch from the band's ends. Measuring with a cloth tape, mark off the ruffle strip into quarters with pins. Then measure and mark the quarters of the band with pins. Align the corresponding pins on the band and the ruffle strip, and pin the two pieces together at those points.

3 Gathering the ruffle. Pull the basting thread at one end of the ruffle strip with one hand; with the other hand distribute the gathers evenly until half of the strip lies ruffled against the band. Repeat at the other end of the strip to gather that half of the fabric into a ruffle. Insert additional pins to secure the ruffle to the band. Then, removing pins as they approach the needle, sew a straight-stitch seam just outside the basting line — ½ inch from the cut edges of ruffle and band — to hold the two pieces together, lock-stitching at the beginning and end of the seam.

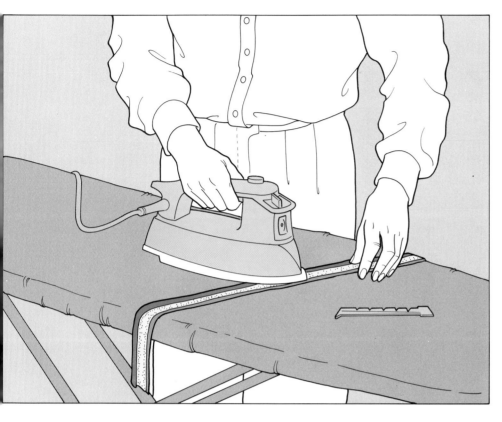

1 **Preparing the pieces.** Follow Step 1, page 80, to figure the length and width of each finished tieback: The one shown here has a 1-inch-wide band and a 2½-inch-wide ruffle. For the ruffle, cut a cross-grain fabric strip 1 inch longer than twice the tieback's finished length and 1 inch wider than twice the finished width *(page 45, Step 3)*. Then follow Steps 4 and 5 on pages 45 and 46 to sew the ruffle strip and run a line of basting stitches along its length.

For the band, cut a fabric strip 1 inch longer than the tieback's finished length and 1 inch wider than twice the band's finished width; then cut a strip of interfacing the tieback's finished length and twice the band's finished width.

Lay the band fabric wrong side up, then measure and press in a ½-inch single hem on one long side. Open the hem and lay a long side of the interfacing, fusible side down, against the crease. Center it along the band's length and fuse the layers together *(page 80, Step 3)*. Close the hem and press with the iron once more *(left)*.

band (wrong side)

stitch line

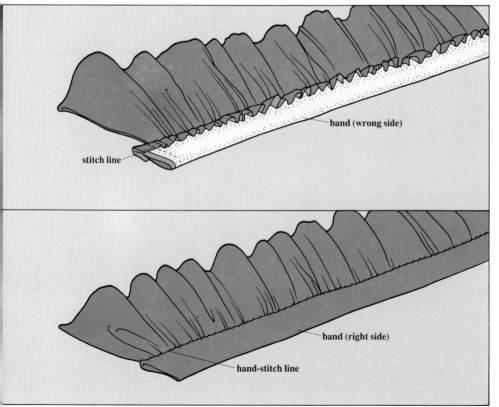

band (right side)

hand-stitch line

4 **Finishing the tieback.** Fold the band back on itself lengthwise, right sides together, as shown in the top picture at left. Pin the fabric together at the band's ends and stitch across the doubled band ½ inch from each end. Turn the band right side out, and hand-stitch the band's folded side to the ruffle *(bottom picture)*. Press lightly with an iron and attach rings to the ends of the band *(page 81, Step 5)*.

A Tieback Support

If curtains are very wide or have been made from an especially heavy fabric, ordinary tiebacks may crush the curtains' outer folds against the wall. Tieback supports that hold those folds away from the wall *(right)* will solve the problem.

A tieback support is a plastic arm that is fastened to the wall inside the curtain's outer edge. The arm extends from 5 to 8 inches to match the length of the curtain's return. The front end of the tieback fastens to a hook on the support's top, and the rear end attaches to a hook on the support's inner face.

Because the front, visible portion of the tieback — the part that reaches from the support's upper hook to the center edge of the curtain — is longer than the part hidden behind the curtain, the tieback is made with a special pattern *(below)*.

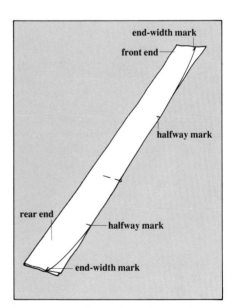

The pattern. Estimate the fabric needed as for a basic tieback *(page 80, Step 1),* but measure around the curtain from the upper to the inner hook. Cut the fabric; fold it lengthwise. Use a pin to indicate the front portion. Pencil marks on the cut edge halfway between the pin and each end. Mark each end as for a basic tieback. Draw curves between the marks, then cut along them.

The support. This tieback support consists of two sections held together by screws and nuts. Loosening the nuts allows one section to slide, changing the support's length. When you find the length that matches the distance of your curtain rod from the wall, tighten the nuts. Attach the support to the wall *(pages 124-125)* at the desired height and just inside the outer edge or return corner of the curtain.

Valances: Soft skirts above the window

Hung from a rod or mounting board above a window, a valance is a short, stationary version of a curtain. It adds a final polish to a window treatment while hiding the curtain rod and its brackets. The miniskirts of the window fashion world, valances are made by the same techniques used for curtains and—like curtains—can be formal or casual, shirred, gathered on a rod or, as shown below, pleated and trimmed with bias tape at top and bottom.

Generally, the valance fabric matches the fabric of the curtains it tops; in this case, both are striped cotton ticking. When a contrast is in order, the valance fabric should weigh at least as much as the curtain fabric to keep the treatment balanced. With solid colors, the fabric grain of the valance must parallel the fabric grain of the curtain; otherwise, they will appear mismatched.

For the most pleasing result, plan a valance one sixth to one seventh the height of the total window treatment. In width, the valance should extend 2 inches beyond the curtain rod on each side to avoid crowding the curtains underneath. And the valance should extend 3 inches farther into the room than the curtains do.

The first step in installing a valance is deciding whether to mount the valance on a board or a curtain rod. You could use a double rod to hold both the curtains and the valance. Here, the curtains are gathered on a straight flat rod, and the valance is mounted on a board that is gently curved for decorative effect *(overleaf)*.

To determine how long a piece of fabric you will need for a pleated valance like this one, divide the finished length of the curtains by six or seven. Add 8 inches for a 4-inch single top hem and a 2-inch double bottom hem. Calculate the width by tripling the width of the area to be covered—that is, the mounting board or rod and the returns. More than likely, you will have to sew together several fabric widths to get this total width *(page 36, Step 2)*. After you join the panels, clip or cut the selvages, press the seams to one side, press in the bottom hem and bind the bottom hemline with bias tape *(Steps 2 and 3)*.

Bias tape, which is prefolded for easy use, comes in dozens of colors, in a variety of widths and in lengths of 3 or 4 yards; it is available wherever fabric is sold. If you prefer, you can make your own tape by cutting bias strips of fabric and joining them as shown on pages 82-83. For special effect, you could also edge the valance with ribbon or braid.

The final construction process is almost exactly like that for making pinch-pleat curtains. Press in double side seams, sew on hem weights, blind-stitch the bottom hem, measure out the finished length and press down the top hem on that line; then insert a buckram heading, add drapery lining *(Step 5)*, and plot and sew the pleats. The exception is that the top and bottom of the valance are encased in tape to give the style symmetry.

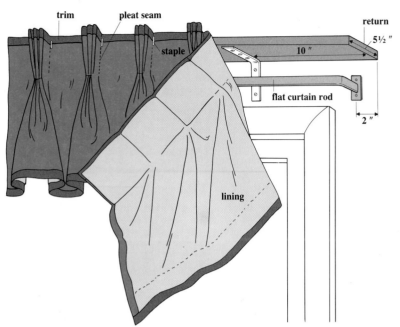

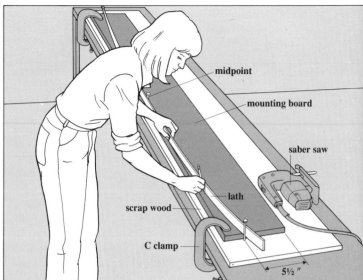

A pinch-pleat valance. Three-fold pleats positioned at equal intervals across the front of a mounting board — in this case, cut in a gentle arc — and at the front corner of each return give this valance a tailored look. Bias tape is sewed on the top and bottom for trim. Staples on both sides of each pleat's seam line hold the valance to the board's front edge. The board is mounted 2 inches above and 2 inches outside a standard flat rod that will hold the curtains. Five-inch angle irons placed 10 inches from each end and at equal distances in between support the board; for strength, their horizontal legs extend almost all the way across the board. Here, the board is nominal 1-by-8 pine lumber, actually ¾ inch thick and 7¼ inches wide — reduced further to curve the front edge.

1 **Making a mounting board.** Place a 1-by-8 of the required length on a piece of scrap wood. Clamp both ends of the board to the worktable. Make tick marks 5½ inches from the far corner on the ends of the board and at the board's midpoint, ¼ inch in from the front edge. At each end mark, drive an eightpenny nail partway into the scrap wood. Drive another eightpenny nail into the board at the midpoint tick mark. Stand a lath strip behind each corner nail and in front of the center nail to form an arc. Draw a pencil along the lath's near edge (*above*). Reclamp the board with its marked edge overhanging the table. Starting at one end, use a saber saw with a medium woodcutting blade to cut along the drawn arc to the midpoint. Cut from the other end in the same way.

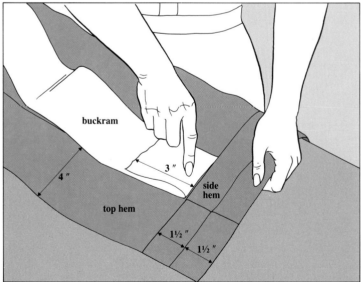

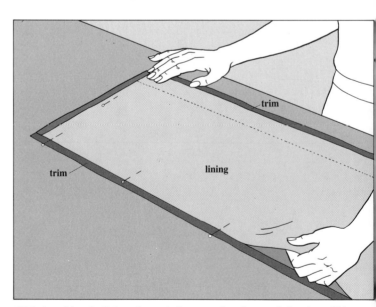

4 **Adding the buckram.** With the top and the side hems unfolded, place the fabric right side down on the worktable. Rip off a strip of 4-inch-wide buckram that is 6 inches longer than the unfinished width of the fabric. Fold back the first 3 inches of buckram at each end. At one end of the fabric, lay the buckram next to the side hem and along the crease for the top hem (*above*). Working across the valance, fold the top hem over the buckram, pinning the hem to the buckram as you go. Then finish the top trim by folding the bias tape over the top hem and blind-stitching it by hand to the wrong side of the fabric. Fold over the side hems and pin them in place.

5 **Attaching the lining.** Cut and piece together drapery lining that will be 1 inch shorter and 1 inch narrower than the fabric. Press in and machine-stitch a 2-inch double bottom hem. Pin and press in a 4-inch single top hem and 1½-inch double side hems; remove the pins. Place the lining over the fabric, wrong side to wrong side. Pin together the lining and fabric at the top and sides (*above*). Then plot and sew pleats using the techniques demonstrated on pages 73-75; make sure each end pleat will fall at the front corner of each return. Hand-stitch the lining to the top corners and sides of the valance fabric, leaving the lining's bottom hem loose.

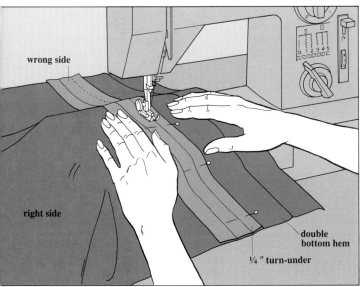

wrong side

right side

double
bottom hem

¼ " turn-under

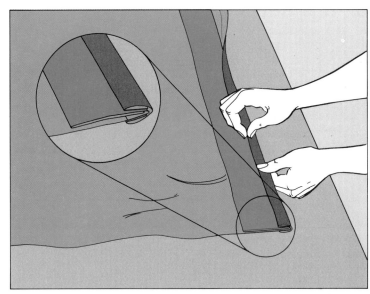

2 **Sewing the trim at the bottom hem.** Cut valance fabric to the required length and width, piecing panels together *(page 36, Step 2)*. Cut a length of 1-inch-wide bias tape equal to the unfinished width of the valance. Press a 2-inch double bottom hem into the valance. Lay the fabric right side up and open out the hem; unfold the bias tape and lay it wrong side up along the bottom crease. Pin the tape to the fabric along the bottom crease line. Then machine-stitch the tape to the fabric about ¼ inch above the crease line, using the crease of the tape's turn-under as a guide *(above)* and removing the pins as you go.

3 **Folding over the trim.** Fold the hem back in place and wrap the bias tape over the bottom crease. Turn the fabric panel over. Fold the raw edge of the tape under *(above)* and pin it down. Press in 1½-inch double side hems. Finish the bottom hem by inserting hem weights *(page 34)* next to each side hem and at the seam lines joining widths of fabric. Blind-stitch the hem and the bias tape in place on the wrong side of the fabric. Then measure up from the finished bottom hem the desired finished length for the valance and press in a 4-inch top hem. Open up the hem and pin bias tape along the crease line on the right side of the fabric in the same way you pinned the tape down on the bottom hem. But do not fold the tape over the hem or sew it yet.

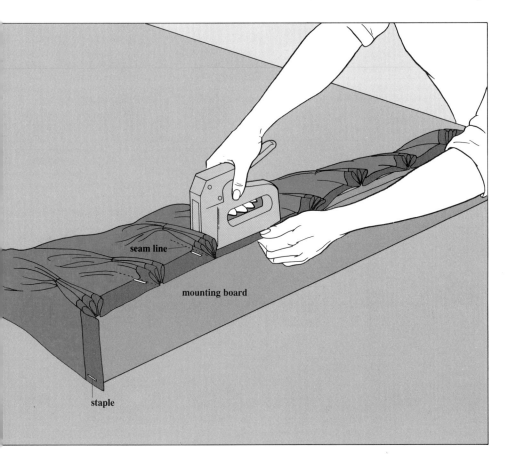

seam line

mounting board

staple

6 **Stapling the valance to the board.** With the valance right side upward, position one end pleat at a front corner and drive a staple into the mounting board on each side of the pleat's stitch line. Staple the valance to the back corner of the board. Then staple the remaining pleats to the board, holding the valance taut. Hide the staples by fluffing out the pleat tops.

Use a straightedge to draw on the wall a line the length of the mounting board and ¾ inch below its desired top height. Screw two 5-inch angle irons into the wall about 10 inches from the ends of the line. Screw more angle irons against the line, evenly spaced between the first pair at about 20-inch intervals. For masonry walls, substitute one of the fasteners on page 125 for the screws.

While a helper steadies the valance on the angle irons, mark on the board's underside the empty screw holes in their horizontal legs. Take down the valance and hammer nails partway into the board at the marked positions to make pilot holes; remove the nails. Reposition the valance and tighten the screws all the way into the holes.

A traditional upholstered cornice

Topping off a curtain with a cornice can give a graceful finishing touch to the framing of a window. Essentially a backless, bottomless box mounted on angle irons emplaced across the top of the window, a cornice can be painted, stained or, as seen here, padded and covered with the same fabric used for the curtains. Its effect is decorative, but a cornice also works to conceal curtain hardware, insulate the window frame and protect the curtains from dust.

Though cornices can be bought ready-made in some sizes at drapery stores or custom-ordered from professional decorators, you can build and upholster your own using only basic carpentry and sewing techniques and tools.

The first step always is to determine the size and design of the box. As a general rule, the height of the cornice face board should be about one fifth or one sixth the height of the total window treatment, measuring from the top of the cornice to the curtain's bottom hem. The face board should cover the stitch line in the curtain pleats, the curtain rods and the top of the window frame. Plan a box whose interior dimensions extend 2 inches beyond the outer edge of the curtains on each side and 3 inches beyond the front face of the

curtain pleats; the latter measurement is particularly important, as curtains that brush against the face board when they are drawn will wear out quickly.

Although a cornice can be a simple rectangle, some ornamental shaping of the face board is usually desirable. Fancy work is dramatic, but simple designs like the one shown here are much easier to upholster. Before deciding on a design, test its effect by cutting it to scale from a piece of kraft paper or cardboard and taping it to the window frame.

The 45-inch-wide cornice here was constructed from sections of ½-inch plywood. Thicker plywood is too unwieldy to upholster. For a narrower window, you could use ¼-inch plywood. Should you opt to paint or stain instead of upholster, use ¾-inch finished lumber.

Whether you have the four components of the box cut to size at a lumberyard or do the job yourself, remember which edges will abut each other when determining the dimensions of the face and side boards. Here, for example, the 14-inch height of the cornice is achieved with a 13½-inch-high face board topped by a ½-inch-thick top — the dust cap. The 6-inch returns are achieved by affixing 5½-inch-long side boards to the ½-inch-thick face board. The pieces are assem-

bled with carpenter's glue and sixpenny finishing nails (Steps 1-3).

The key to a professional-looking upholstered cornice lies in smoothing and fitting the cover fabric over a layer of padding. Stable, tightly woven fabrics work best; open-weave and sheer fabrics may stretch too much. Polyester batting that has been cut from a roll makes the most satisfactory padding; cotton padding can get lumpy, and any padding sold in folded form may retain unsightly crease marks that may show through the cover fabric.

Typically, a cornice is covered with the same fabric as the curtains it tops. Printed fabrics camouflage slight errors of fit better than solid colors, but you must make sure that the print is centered on the face and side boards and matches at the front corners. If this involves joining panels of fabric (page 36, Step 2), center one panel on the front board so that the piecing seams fall symmetrically.

Solid fabrics can be turned sideways to avoid seams — a process called railroading. Some railroaded fabrics may take on a slightly different shading, but with solids the color difference is usually less conspicuous than seam lines would be.

Whatever fabric you choose, it should be cut to a rectangle that is 6 inches greater than the height of the cornice and 6

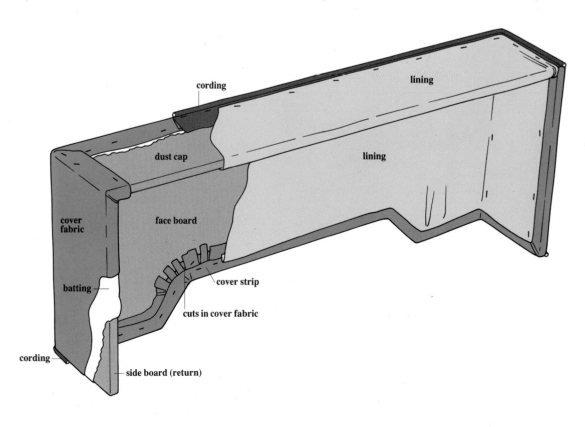

cording

dust cap

lining

lining

cover
fabric

face board

cover strip

batting

cuts in cover fabric

cording

side board (return)

nches greater than the distance from the back of one side around the face board to the back of the opposite side. You must also allow for an extra 2½-inch-wide strip of cover fabric that will wrap around the cornice's lower edge to hide the scissor cuts and stapling that will pull the fabric taut *(Step 8),* as well as for two 2½-inch-wide strips of material for the cording along the cornice edges *(Step 10).* Here, the cording strips are cut from a solid-colored fabric to accent the cover fabric's print. The cording material is sewed around lengths of ¼-inch nylon cord, then secured along the cornice's top and bottom edges.

To finish the cornice, buy a rectangular section of cotton broadcloth drapery lining large enough to cover the interior of the box and the exterior of the dust cap.

The completed box is mounted on angle irons screwed in position over the window. Choose angle irons whose horizontal legs extend almost all the way across the underside of the dust cap. Allow one angle iron for every 20 inches or fraction thereof in the cornice width.

Although you will want to train the pleats of your curtains before the cornice is mounted, it is then usually easier to remove the curtains, mount the cornice and rehang the curtains.

An upholstered cornice. The ½-inch plywood frame — seen at left from the rear — consists of four pieces: a decoratively shaped face board, two side boards or returns, and a top board or dust cap. Cushioning is provided by a layer of polyester batting invisible beneath the cover fabric. The cover fabric is smoothed across the face board and the returns, then stapled in place inside the box and at the edge of the top of the dust cap. Cording runs along the top and bottom edges. At the box's lower edge, a cover strip attached to the lower cording conceals the cuts and staples that make the fabric taut. Drapery lining, fitted and stapled in place, covers the box interior and the top of the dust cap.

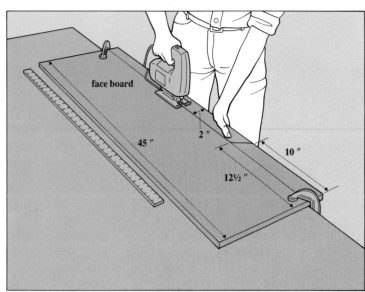

1 **Marking and cutting the face-board design.** Using a yardstick or carpenter's square, draw a pencil line across the face board 2 inches from what will be its lower edge. Make a pair of tick marks on the lower edge of the board 10 inches from each end and another pair on the pencil line 12½ inches from each end. Connect the pairs of adjacent tick marks with diagonal lines. With C clamps, fasten the board to a worktable, letting the board's marked edge overhang the table. Fit a blade for plywood into a saber saw and cut into the board along one diagonal line, across the midsection of the line parallel to the edge and back to the edge along the opposite diagonal. Remove the clamps.

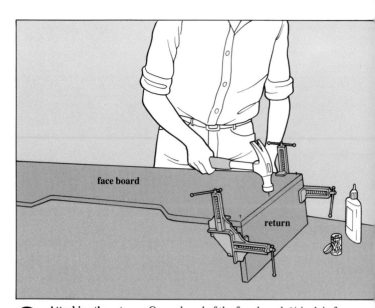

2 **Attaching the returns.** On each end of the face board, ¼ inch in from the edge, mark locations for nails ¾ inch from the top and bottom and squarely in between. Start sixpenny finishing nails at the marked locations by driving the nails partway through the plywood. On one return board, spread a bead of wood glue along the edge that will butt against the end of the face board. Align the return's outer face flush with the end of the face board and hold the pieces together with corner clamps while you finish driving the nails in the face board into the return. Remove the corner clamps. Secure the other return to the opposite end of the face board in the same way.

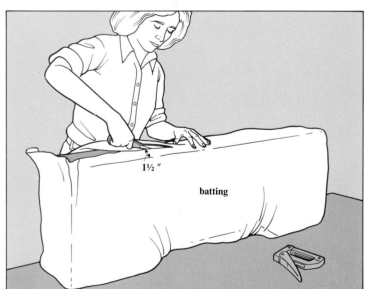

4 **Padding the box.** Smooth the corners and edges of the box with medium (120-grit) sandpaper. Cut a piece of lightweight polyester batting long enough to cover the front and sides generously. With the box standing upright, wrap the batting around the cornice, and trim it to about 1½ inches wider than the cornice's height (*above*). The batting will cling to the wood by itself. Secure the batting by shooting a single staple through it into the dust cap near the center of the cap's front edge.

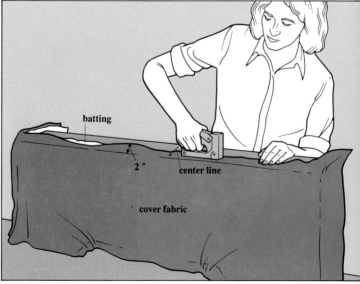

5 **Centering the cover fabric.** Mark the center of the dust cap at its front edge. Press the cut rectangle of cover fabric lightly with a steam iron to rid it of wrinkles. Fold it in half end to end and insert a pin at the center of its top edge. Unfold the cover fabric and hold it against the front of the box, aligning the pin on the fabric with the center line on the dust cap; let the fabric overlap the dust cap by about 2 inches. Staple the fabric to the center of the dust cap, remove the pin and continue stapling at about 7-inch intervals toward one end of the dust cap (*above*).

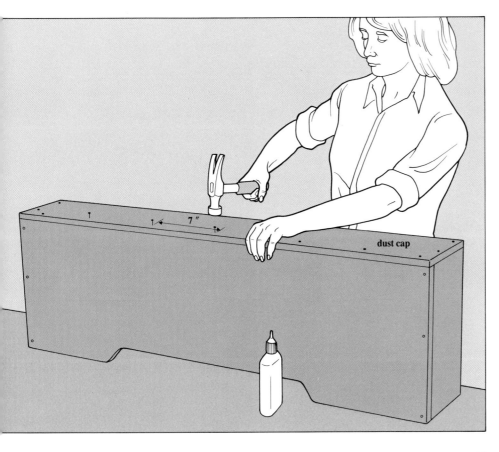

3 **Attaching the dust cap.** Start sixpenny finishing nails along the ends and what will be the front edge of the dust cap, positioning them ¼ inch in from the edge: Space two nails at each end and locate nails in the front edge 2 inches from the ends and at about 7-inch intervals in between. Apply a line of wood glue to the top edges of the returns and face board. Align the edges of the dust cap flush with the exterior of the frame; drive in the nails.

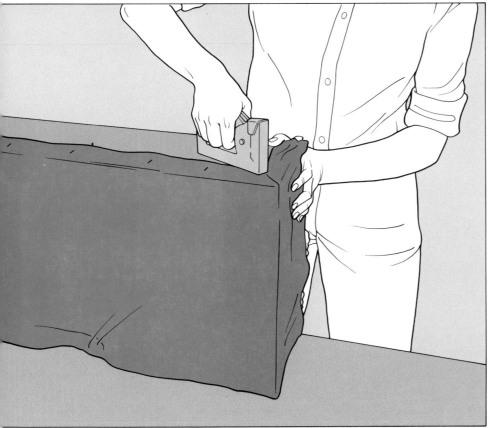

6 **Folding the top corner.** At the front corner of the dust cap, fold the excess fabric to form a mitered corner. Staple the fabric in place at the corner *(left)* and along the end of the dust cap. Starting again at the center of the dust cap, work along the front edge and around the opposite end in the same way, gently smoothing the fabric and stapling it in place as you go. ▶

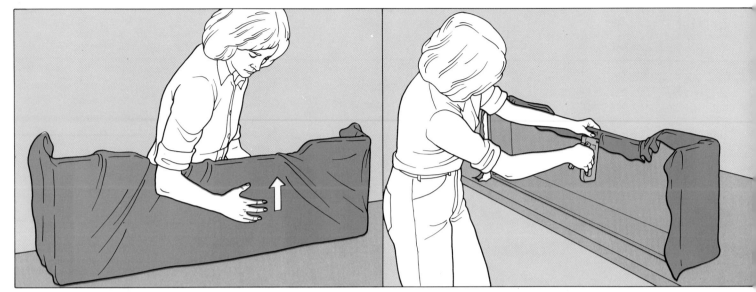

7 **Attaching fabric along the lower edge.** Turn the box upside down so that it rests on the dust cap. Working at the center of the box *(above, left)*, smooth the fabric and batting gently upward *(arrow)*. Wrap the excess around the inside edge of the face board. Holding the fabric at the center taut against the back of the face board without stretching it, drive staples through the fabric to secure it *(above, right)*. Work from the center toward one corner along the middle section of the decorative cutout, smoothing and stapling the fabric frequently as you go.

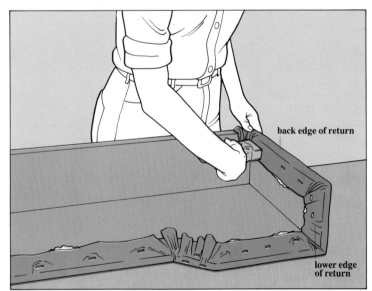

9 **Covering the returns.** Place the box on its face. Pull the excess fabric and batting taut at the center of the lower edge of one return, and staple the fabric in place. If necessary, take tucks and make mitered folds at the corners of the lower edge so that the fabric can be stapled smoothly. Staple the fabric along the back edge of the return and around the top corner. Secure the fabric and batting around the opposite return in the same way. Trim away any excess flaps of fabric or batting along the back of the face board where you have made cuts to ease the fabric.

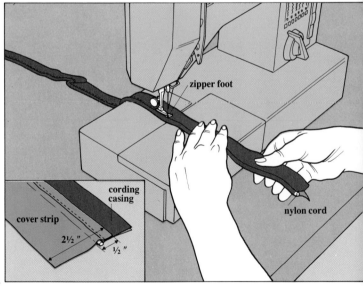

10 **Sewing cording strips.** Cut three strips of fabric 2½ inches wide and 3 inches longer than the entire bottom edge of the cornice. Cut two strips from solid-colored fabric for the cording, and one from the cover fabric. Cut a section of ¼-inch nylon cord to the strip length. Center the cord on one strip and fold the fabric over it. Replace your sewing machine's presser foot with a zipper-foot attachment. Guide the cord and fabric under the zipper foot *(above)*, with the cord just to the left of the foot. Prepare and sew a second cording strip similarly. Sew the strip of cover fabric wrong side up along one of the finished cording strips, positioning the cover strip so that one edge overlaps the encased cord by about ½ inch *(inset)*.

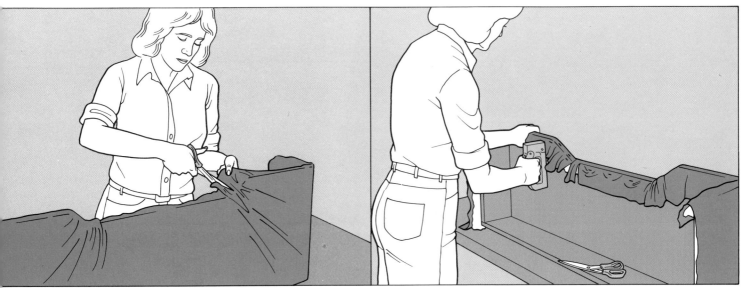

8 **Fitting the fabric around the design.** To ease the fabric around the angled section of the cutout and avoid puckering across the front of the face board, cut slits into the excess fabric that wraps around the edge *(above, left)*. As you proceed, staple the fabric in place up to and even across the face board's edge *(above, right)*; this will pull the material taut across the front. Smooth the fabric continuously, and do not hesitate to cut and staple it: The lower cording and cover strip — which will be attached later along the edge of the face board — will hide any staples or slits. Do not be concerned about small wrinkles along the front: You

will pull them taut when you secure the fabric around the returns. After working along the face board to one return, start at the center of the box once more and fit the fabric around the other angle of the cutout, along the face board to the opposite return.

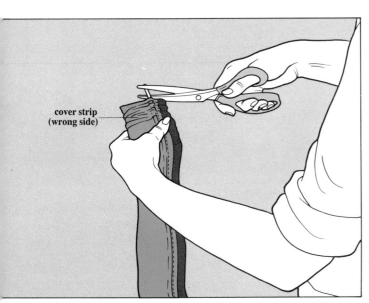

cover strip
(wrong side)

11 **Making a hollow casing.** Orient the cording strip that has the strip of cover fabric sewed to it so that the cover strip faces wrong side up and extends to the left. This strip will be used along the lower edge of the cornice. At the top end of the assembly, pull the casing back to expose 1 inch of cord. Cut off the exposed cord to create a 1-inch-long hollow casing. Then prepare 1 inch of hollow casing at one end of the top cording strip, which has no cover strip attached.

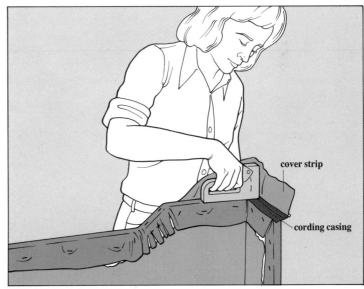

cover strip

cording casing

12 **Stapling the lower cording.** Stand the cornice upside down. Position the hollow-casing end of the lower cording strip so that the end of the cord aligns with the end of the right return and the cording is flush with the return's outside face. The excess fabric from the casing should lie across the edge of the return while the cover strip extends upward. Drive staples into the edge of the return behind the cording, along the seam that attaches the cover strip *(above)*. Manipulate the cording around the corner and work along the front. Before stapling the cording to the opposite return, trim it so that there is only 1 inch of excess and prepare 1 inch of hollow casing at the trimmed end. Then staple the cording along the return. ▶

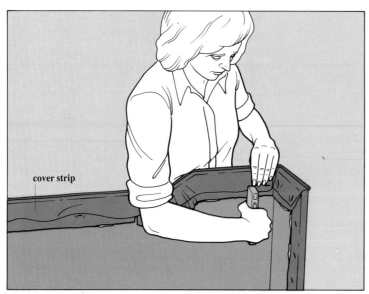

13 **Securing the cover strip along the lower edge.** Fold the section of hollow casing at a 90° angle across the back edge of one return. Hold the casing in place by pulling the attached cover strip across the edge and onto the back of the return. Turn under the end of the cover strip and staple it in place along the back of the return. Continue to pull and staple the cover strip in place along the return, then along the back of the face board *(above)*, tucking in excess fabric at the corners where the face board and returns intersect. Secure the cover strip along the back of the opposite return in the same way.

14 **Attaching the top cording.** Turn the cornice right side up. Position the hollow-casing end of the top cording strip so that the end of the cord aligns with the back edge of the dust cap and the cording lies flush with the outer face of the return. Drive staples into the dust cap along the cording seam to secure the cording. Fold the excess casing neatly at the corner and continue stapling the cording along the front edge of the dust cap. Before stapling it to the opposite return, trim the cording so that it has 1 inch of hollow casing at its end. Staple the cording along the opposite return. Tuck the hollow casing at each end neatly under itself to complete the top cording.

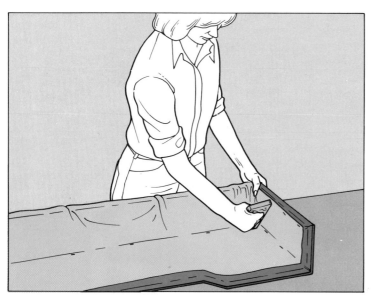

17 **Lining the interior.** Flip the lining back into the box, pulling it gently to smooth it along the stapled lower edge. Working from the center of the box toward one end, smooth the lining across the back of the face board. Place staples at 8- to 10-inch intervals where the face board and dust cap meet. When you reach the corner, staple along the intersection of the face board and return, then tuck any excess lining under itself and staple along the back edge of the return *(above)* so that the return is neatly lined. Secure the lining to the inside of the other half of the box in the same way.

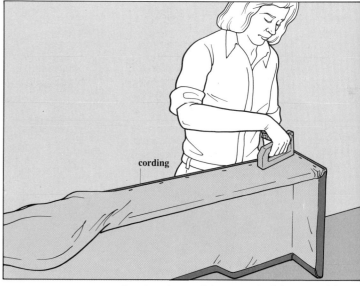

18 **Lining the top.** Stand the box upright. Wrap the lining around the back edge and across the exterior face of the dust cap. Trim the lining so that about 2 inches extends beyond the front of the box. Starting at the center of the dust cap and working toward one end, smooth the lining in place and tuck the excess under so that the lining extends neatly all the way to the cording on the front edge. Staple the lining in place along the front edge at 3- to 4-inch intervals as you go. At the end of the dust cap, fold any excess lining under and staple it neatly in place *(above)*. Staple lining to the other half of the dust cap in the same way.

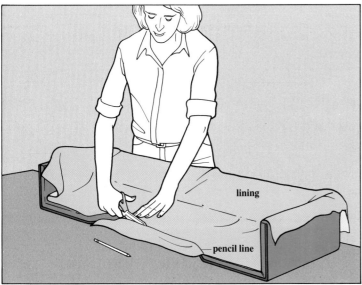

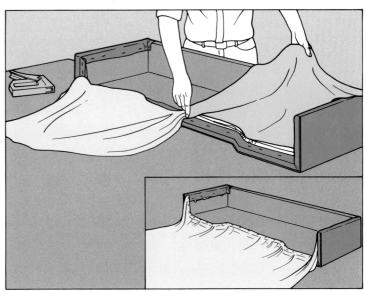

15 **Cutting the lining to fit.** Cut a rectangle of drapery lining large enough to cover the inside of the face board, returns and dust cap and the top of the dust cap. Allow a margin of 6 inches for each of these dimensions. With the cornice resting on its face, spread the lining evenly inside it, with one lining edge along the lower edge of the box. Use a pencil to trace the design along the lower edge onto the lining. Then cut the lining along the marked design *(above)*.

16 **Reversing and stapling the lining.** Pull the lining back so that the section you cut out to match the face-board design lies about 1 inch inside the edge of the box. With your index finger holding the lining's front edge at the center of the cutout section, flip the lining out of the box onto the worktable with your other hand *(above)*. Then, starting in the center (where your finger is holding the lining in place) and working toward one return, staple the edge of the lining to the back of the face board about 1 inch in from the board's edge. Continue stapling the lining up the back of the return. Then go back to the center and work toward the opposite return so that the lining is secured along the box's entire lower edge *(inset)*.

19 **Mounting the cornice box.** Screw three 5-inch angle irons on a level line above the window so that their horizontal legs lie ¾ inch below the height you have chosen for the mounted cornice. Have a helper steady the cornice on the angle irons while you mark the positions of the screw holes in the horizontal legs on the underside of the dust cap *(right)*. Take the cornice down and hammer pilot holes at the marked positions. Reposition the cornice and secure it to the angle irons with screws.

An array
of decorative
shades

The basic job of a shade or blind is to provide a quick and easy way to cover or uncover a window. But many models add much more, bringing a color or pattern to a room, or even helping to insulate it from heat and cold. In any case, your selection need not be limited to the common roller shade or venetian blind. This chapter shows you how to make shades in a variety of decorative styles, from the simplicity of fabric-laminated roller shades to the graceful opulence of balloon shades.

A shade, which is a single flexible panel that rolls or folds away from the window, may be made of opaque material that lets you block out almost all light when drawn; you can also make a shade from a translucent material that filters and softens the light. A blind has louvers that can be adjusted to different angles to regulate the exact amount of light that passes, from almost none to almost all.

Most shades and blinds are suspended from the top of the window by brackets, which can be attached inside the window opening or outside on the window frame or wall. An inside installation presents a clean, spare appearance; it is most efficient for blocking light and trapping a layer of air next to the window to insulate against heat or cold. An outside installation, useful in creating the illusion of a wider window, becomes necessary if the opening is not deep enough for an inside mount.

For most shades and blinds, the window recess must be at least 2 inches deep to allow an inside installation. This provides clearance for the roller or headrail (the rigid top piece of a blind that conceals the lifting mechanism). You may need even more depth if the shade is particularly long or made from a heavy fabric, which will produce a bulky roll at the top when the shade is raised. Vertical blinds *(page 100)* require a recess as deep as the width of one louver — about 4 inches. For an inside installation of a shade or blind, choose a width that leaves a clearance of no more than ¼ inch on each side; for an outside mount, the measurements are less critical, but you should allow at least 1 inch of overlap on each side of the window opening to reduce light leaks and ensure privacy.

Ready-made shades and blinds are available at department stores and home-supply centers. Roller shades often come in widths that can easily be trimmed in ¼- to ½-inch increments to fit any number of window sizes. Pleated shades, roman shades and venetian blinds are available in widths that range from 18 to 56 inches, and in lengths from 42 to 72 inches. Ready-made vertical blinds usually come in only one size — 84 inches, to fit sliding glass doors; window-width vertical blinds must be custom-made.

If the shade or blind you want is not available in the size you need, you can probably place a special order through the store or a custom window-covering shop. Custom-made shades and blinds are a bit more expensive than the ready-made variety, but they usually incorporate higher-quality materials.

The examples on the following pages illustrate the types of hardware used to mount five popular styles of shades and blinds. With the exception of roller-shade hardware, which is sold separately, mounting brackets and installation instructions should be included with any shades or blinds you buy. The bracket shapes may vary slightly from those shown here, but the mounting principles are similar. If you make your own roman shades *(pages 104-111),* you will have to buy angle irons to install them.

You can install most brackets with the small nails or screws supplied with the shades, but you may need to substitute different fasteners *(page 125)* if you are mounting the brackets on a material other than wood. In most cases you will need a drill to make small starter holes for screws, but a hammer may be all you need to nail brackets for a lightweight shade in wood.

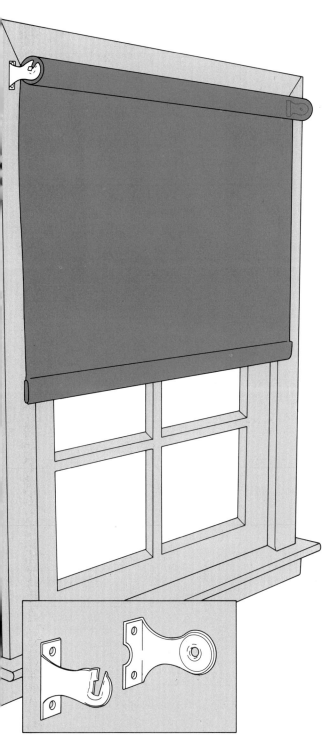

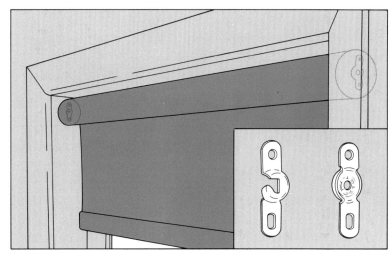

Conventional inside mount. For an installation inside the window opening, small flat brackets *(inset, above)* are screwed or nailed to the side jambs with enough clearance below the top of the window to allow room for the shade to roll freely.

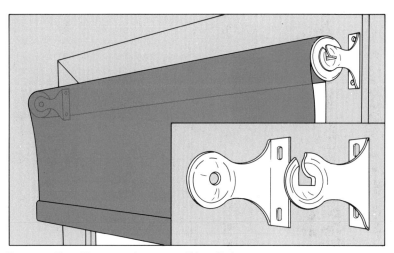

Reverse-roll outside mount. A reverse-roll installation turns a conventional shade end for end so that the fabric falls over the front of the roller. The slotted bracket thus must be on the right; for a reverse-roll outside mount like this, special brackets *(inset, above)* are required.

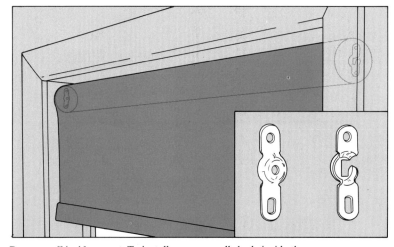

Reverse-roll inside mount. To install a reverse-roll shade inside the opening for the window, you can use standard flat brackets, simply reversing their position on the window jamb so that the slotted bracket is on the right-hand side *(inset, above)*.

Roller shades. For the conventional outside mount shown here, the shade fabric descends behind the roller, which is supported by two brackets *(inset)*. The round pin on the right-hand end of the roller turns in the hole of its matching bracket; the flat pin on the left-hand end is kept from turning by the flat slot of its bracket. The flat pin attaches inside the roller to a spring, which tightens as the shade is drawn; the spring tension, when released by a ratchet mechanism at the end of the roller, provides the power to roll the shade up.

Roman shades. A roman shade is attached to its mounting board *(page 108)* before the board is installed. The mounting board is supported by a pair of angle irons with legs that are 1½ inches long.

To mount the shade outside the window opening *(right)*, first center the board atop the window. Make tick marks on the wall or window frame at each end of the board and screw one leg of each angle iron ½ inch inside each mark. Center the mounting board on the angle irons and screw the legs to the board.

To mount a shade inside the window opening *(inset)*, hold the shade against the top jamb and position one leg of an angle iron at the center of each end of the mounting board, and the other leg against the side jamb. Mark the screw holes on the board and the jamb. Screw one leg of each angle iron to the side jamb, slide the shade into place and screw the other leg to the board. For clarity, no shade is shown attached to the mounting board here.

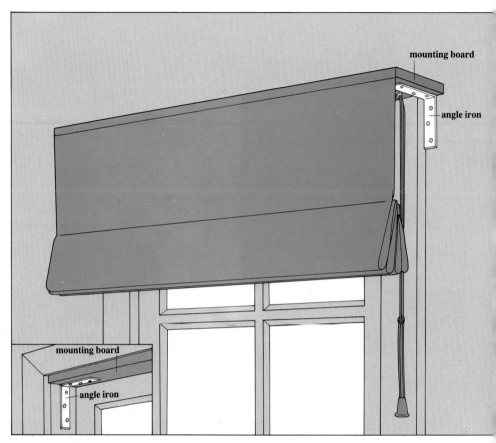

Vertical blinds. The headrail of a vertical blind is supported at the ends and center by swivel brackets. When the bracket's lever is turned to a closed position, prongs protruding from it engage slots in the top of the headrail, locking the headrail in place.

For an inside mount *(right)*, each swivel bracket is screwed to the top jamb through the center of the bracket *(top inset)*; the screw should be just loose enough so the lever can swivel under mild pressure.

For an outside mount, *(bottom inset)*, each swivel bracket is attached to an angle iron with a self-tapping screw. The angle iron is then secured to the wall or the window frame with screws.

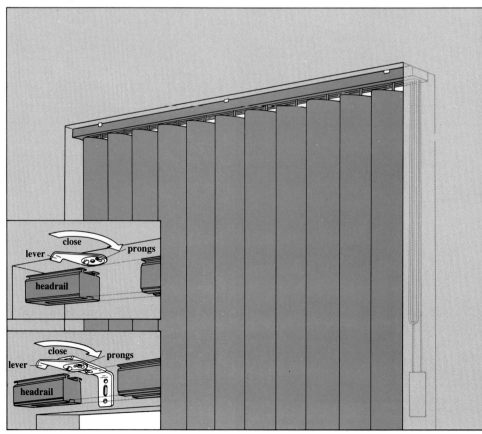

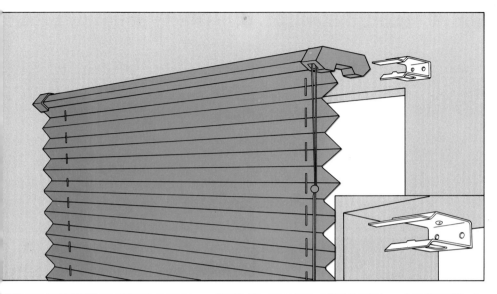

Pleated shades. The headrail of a pleated shade is supported near each end by a snap-in bracket. For an outside mount *(left)*, attach the bracket to the wall or the window frame with screws through holes in the back of the bracket.

For an inside mount *(inset)*, attach the bracket to the window jamb with screws through holes in the top of the bracket. Center the shade over the opening and push the headrail into the brackets; the brackets engage the headrail with a sharp click.

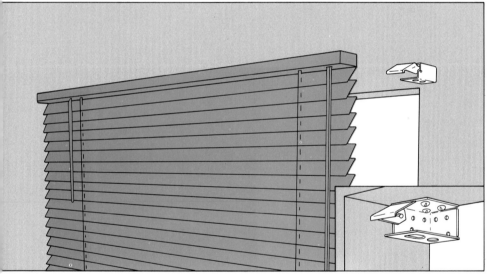

Venetian blinds. The headrails of all widths of venetian blinds are supported at their ends by brackets of similar design. To install the blind outside the window opening *(left)*, drive screws through the holes in the back of the brackets into the window frame or the wall.

To install the blind inside the window opening *(inset)*, drive screws through holes in the top of the bracket into the top window jamb. Install the blind by pushing it into the brackets and snapping the hinged cap over the front of the blind.

Leveling a Shade

Wherever a shade or blind is mounted, inside the window frame or outside, it must be level. To accomplish this, first fit the brackets on the shade and center the shade on the window frame where it will hang. Mark the screw holes of one bracket, take down the shade and install that bracket. Fit the shade into the installed bracket. While a helper holds a level atop the shade, move the shade's free end until the level's bubble is centered; mark the screw holes of the other bracket and install it. Then hang the shade.

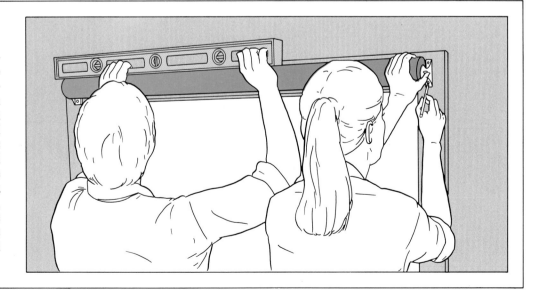

Making a fabric-covered roller shade

Dressing up a window with an attractive roller shade is a quick, economical way to brighten a dull room. Though stock shades can be purchased in a variety of colors and patterns, with only a little extra effort you can custom-make your own — simply by ironing your choice of fabric onto a special adhesive-coated backing.

Little sewing is involved and — besides the fabric and the backing — the only materials you need are a wood roller (which comes with a slat to weight the shade), a pull and appropriate mounting hardware.

Working on a large table with a few basic tools, you can make a roller shade like the one here in less than two hours.

Choose a tightly woven medium-weight fabric that will withstand the moderately high heat required to melt the adhesive on the backing. Cotton was used here, but cotton-polyester blends are also good. Avoid stain-resistant fabrics; their special finishes will interfere with the bonding. There is no need to prewash the fabric, but do press it before you begin.

The woven iron-on backing comes with a peel-off protective paper over its adhesive side. It is available at many fabric stores in 36- and 54-inch-wide rolls, i both translucent and opaque styles. Fus ible web, another iron-on product, is les expensive but lacks the woven backing' strength, durability and consistency.

Buy enough backing to cover th shade's finished length — the length of th window opening plus 18 inches. To deter mine the finished width — the width t which you should cut the backing — firs mount your brackets and level them, us ing a yardstick and a level, then measur the distance between the parts that wi hold the ends of the roller; subtract ½ inch for clearance. Because the joinin of fabric and backing makes a slightl bulkier shade than the store-bought vari ety, for an outside mount you shoul get extra-large hardware; for an insid mount, the standard hardware should b positioned 1½ inches below the jamb.

Having cut a rectangle of backing to th shade's finished dimensions, measur and cut a rectangle of fabric 2 inches long er and 2 inches wider than the backing This way, when you prepare to join th fabric to the backing *(Step 2)*, the fabri will overlap by 1 inch on all sides.

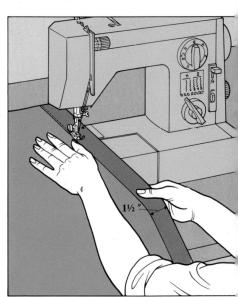

3 **Sewing the slat casing.** When the shade has cooled, and while it is still face down on the table, use a hemming gauge or ruler as a guide to turn back one end 1½ inches. Pre the turned-back end lightly with the iron, creasing it to form the slat casing. Pinning is unnecessary. Machine-stitch the casing, ¼ inch from the raw edge, using eight stitches to the inch and lock-stitching both ends of the seam. Slide the slat into the casing.

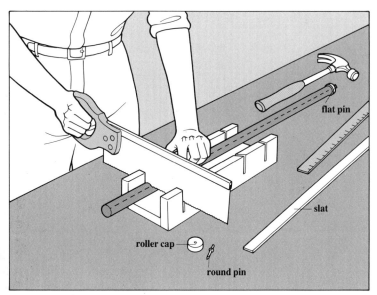

flat pin

slat

roller cap

round pin

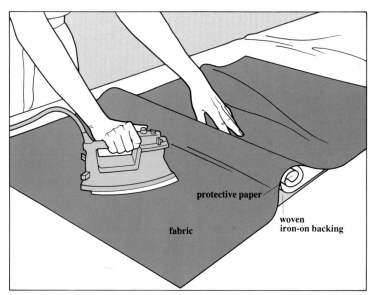

protective paper

fabric

woven
iron-on backing

1 Cutting the roller to size. Measure between mounted brackets and subtract ⅛ inch. Mark this distance on the roller, measuring from the flat-pin end but excluding the pin from the measurement. Remove the roller cap and round pin from the opposite end. Using a miter box and backsaw to ensure a square cut, saw the roller at the mark *(above)*. Fit the cap on the cut end and drive the round pin home with a hammer. Then mark and saw the wood slat, used to weight the shade, to the same length less ⅜ inch. If the roller does not have a guideline to indicate where the shade should be stapled *(Step 5)*, draw one yourself: Hold the roller firmly on the worktable, lay a pencil on the table with its point touching the roller, and slide the pencil along the roller's entire length.

2 Bonding the fabric to the backing. Spread a bedsheet over the table to provide light padding. Lay the backing, paper side up, on the sheet. Roll back the protective paper from the first 18 inches of backing. Lay the fabric right side up over the exposed backing so that 1 inch of fabric overlaps all around. Using a dry iron set at the appropriate setting for the fabric, iron the fabric onto the backing, working from the center outward. Move the iron very slowly, lingering 10 to 15 seconds over each section of the fabric. Continue working in 18-inch increments — rolling back the paper as you proceed — to the end of the fabric. Let the sandwich of fabric and backing cool for 30 minutes, then turn it over, cover it with the protective paper and iron again. Trim the excess fabric.

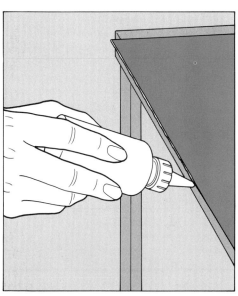

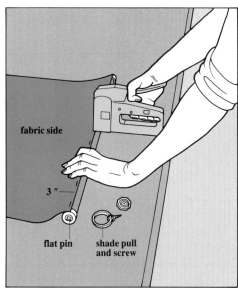

fabric side

3 "

flat pin

shade pull
and screw

4 Protecting edges from fraying. Lay the shade flat on the table, with one side extending ½ inch over a table edge. Working in 10-inch increments, apply a bead of white household glue along one side of the shade; wipe off the excess by drawing a clean, dry cloth toward you across the edge of the shade. Glue the other side in the same way.

5 Assembling the shade. Lay the roller on the table with the flat pin on your left and the guideline up. Lay the shade on the table, fabric side up for a reverse roll or fabric side down for a conventional roll. Center the unhemmed end of the shade atop the roller, align it with the guideline, then use a staple gun to staple the shade to the roller at 3-inch intervals. Screw the shade pull into a starter hole at the midpoint of the slat. Roll up the shade.

6 Adjusting the shade. Hang the shade by inserting the roller pins into their matching brackets. Draw the shade and let it roll up. If the shade does not roll to the top of the window, take it down and tighten the spring inside the roller by rolling up 12 inches of shade by hand *(above)*; then replace the shade in its brackets and roll it up again. If the shade rolls up too quickly, unroll 12 inches by hand. Continue testing until the shade rolls up and down satisfactorily.

The roman style: Efficiency with flair

Flat when released, but collected into accordion-like pleats when raised, the roman shade always has a crisp, tailored look. The absence of tucks and gathers shows off an attractive fabric pattern to advantage and spells economy as well: A roman shade needs only one third to one half the fabric a curtain would require to cover the same window.

Although tension rods and roller mounts are sometimes used, the shade is normally mounted on a 1-by-2 pine board that fits snug inside the window frame, as seen here, or rests on angle irons screwed to the wall above the window *(page 100)*. For either position, the shade can be lined *(Steps 3-4)*, which will not only protect the shade fabric from fading in the sun, but add body to the pleats, help insulate the room, and filter out street noise. If you buy lining with a coated backing, make sure the backing faces the windowpane. Otherwise, use muslin or a tightly woven cotton broadcloth.

The shade is raised and lowered by nylon cords threaded through ⅜-inch rings that are sewed to the back of the lining in evenly spaced horizontal rows and vertical columns *(right)*. Ready-made shade tape with plastic rings attached to it is available at sewing stores and fabric centers, but individual bone or brass rings cost less, require less stitching and let you determine the pleat width — which is always equal to half the distance between horizontal rows of rings.

On the mounting board, each cord passes through a ½-inch screw eye located above each column of rings. The cords run horizontally through the screw eyes toward one side of the shade, where they join to form a single draw cord. With heavy or unusually wide shades, the cords should be given extra support on the pull side with an extra screw eye or a small pulley attached to the board.

The draw cord is tethered to a small awning cleat installed out of view on the jamb inside the window frame. To provide enough weight for the shade to be lowered evenly, a ⅜-inch metal rod cut ½ inch shorter than the shade's finished width is inserted in a rod casing sewed at the bottom of the shade *(Step 5)*.

Because a roman shade must form a perfect rectangle, use a tightly woven fabric whose dimensions will remain stable — chintz, for example, or chambray. The grain of the fabric will determine how the shade will hang, so make sure that the grain is straight and that the fabric pattern — if any — is aligned with the grain *(pages 18-19)*.

Allow for 1½-inch double side hems and a 4-inch double bottom hem to give a measure of firmness to the edges. For shades that require more than a single width of fabric, first sew equal strips of fabric to either side of a center strip. Then cut off the raw edges within ¼ inch of the seams and press the seam allowances to one side.

To cover the mounting board, you will need an additional piece of fabric that is 3 inches longer than the board and about 6 inches wide. For an inside mount, you can use less expensive lining fabric; for an outside mount, you will need face fabric because the mounting-board cover will be visible inside the room.

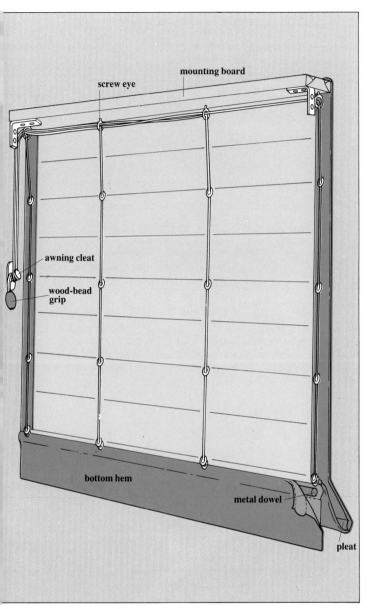

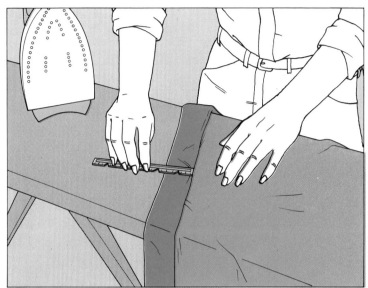

Rear view of a roman shade. The shade owes its trim, neat look to a ring-and-cord system hidden from view on the shade's rear side. Individual cords are threaded through screw eyes in the mounting board, then down through each column of rings. The cords are joined at one side to form a single draw cord, which is tipped with a wood bead grip. As the shade is drawn up, the fabric folds in orderly pleats along horizontal lines midway between adjacent rows of rings. It is held in place by wrapping the draw cord around an awning cleat attached inside the window jamb. A metal rod concealed in a casing sewed into the bottom *(cutaway)* makes the shade hang evenly.

1 **Forming the double side hems.** Cut the fabric for the shade 7 inches longer than its finished length and 6 inches wider than its finished width; if necessary, piece the fabric to produce these dimensions. Spread the fabric wrong side up on a flat work surface. Working down one side of the fabric, fold inward a 1½-inch strip for a side hem. For accuracy, measure the fold with a hemming gauge *(above)*. Adjust the fold as necessary, then crease the strip with a steam iron. Continue to fold, measure and crease until you reach the bottom. Then fold over the creased strip another 1½ inches and press it to form a double hem. Pin the side hem in place at 6-inch intervals. Repeat the process on the other side of the fabric to form the second double side hem.

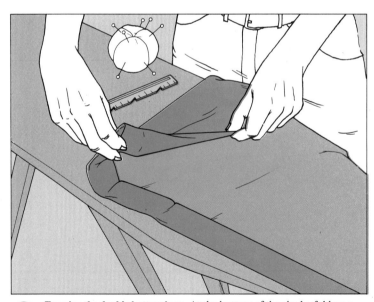

2 **Forming the double bottom hem.** At the bottom of the shade, fold up a 1-inch single hem and press it with the steam iron. Fold up the single hem 4 inches *(above)*. Measure it with the hemming gauge and crease it along the fold with the iron. Pin the double bottom hem in place. ▶

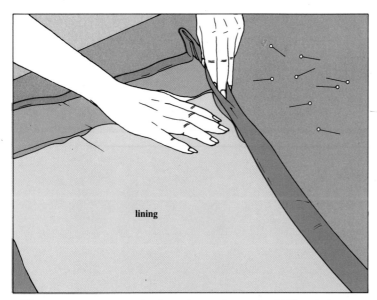

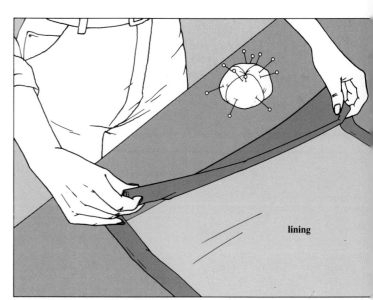

3 **Positioning the lining.** Unpin the bottom hem and unfold its 4-inch panel. Unpin the side hems but do not unfold them. Position the lining on the back of the shade: An insulated backing must face upward. Slip the edges of the lining under the side hems *(above)*. Make sure the bottom edge of the lining does not extend past the crease made by the 4-inch bottom hem. Now smooth out the lining with your hands, and pin each side hem to the lining at 6-inch intervals.

4 **Joining the lining to the shade.** Refold the bottom hem *(above)* and pin it in place. Cut off the excess lining that protrudes above the top of the shade fabric so that the two pieces are of equal length; take care not to cut off any of the shade fabric in the process. Using a wide zigzag stitch *(page 22)*, sew the top edges of both the lining and the fabric together to prevent their cut edges from unraveling.

7 **Marking ring placement on lining.** Divide the distance between the two bottom dots by 8; if the result contains a fraction, round the result up to the next whole number. Then divide the shade's finished width by that number to determine how far apart the columns should be spaced. Now align each pair of opposite dots with the edge of a yardstick or metal tape measure, and mark dots on the lining between them at the interval you calculated above. Make sure all dots align vertically and horizontally.

   For shades less than 24 inches wide, align each pair of opposite dots, and mark a dot on the lining halfway between them.

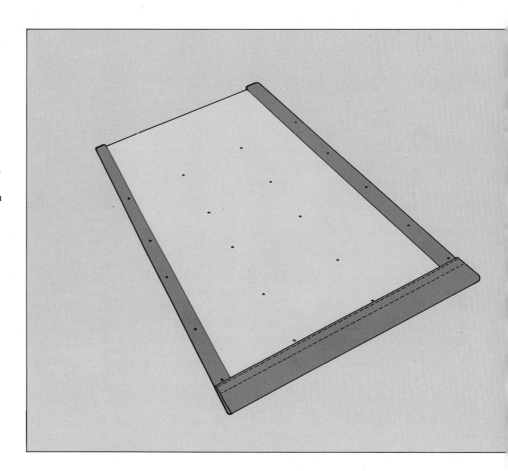

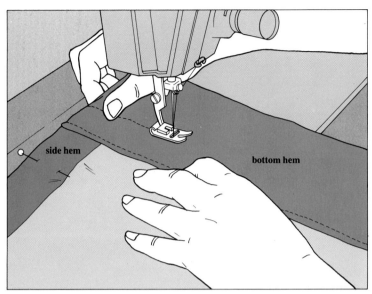

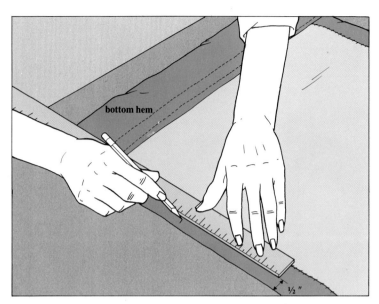

5 **Making the rod casing.** Using thread the same color as the fabric, straight-stitch the bottom hem by sewing along the fold made by the 1-inch single hem. To keep the hem in place, leave the pins in until you come to them. Begin and end the stitch line with lock stitching *(page 21)*. To form the rod casing, sew a second straight-stitch line *(above)* that is parallel to the first but 1 inch closer to the bottom of the shade. Using a blind-hem stitch *(page 23)*, sew the side hems in place, working from the bottom of the fabric to the top and removing the pins as you go.

6 **Determining ring placement.** Just above the rod casing's top stitch line, make a pencil or chalk mark ½ inch from the edge of a side hem. Measuring from that mark and working from the bottom of the shade toward the top, mark dots ½ inch in from the edge at intervals that are twice the intended pleat width of the shade. For 2½-inch pleats, for example, mark the dots at 5-inch intervals; for 4-inch pleats, which will match the width of the bottom hem, mark them at 8-inch intervals. Do not mark any dots within two pleat widths plus 2 inches of the top of the shade fabric. Mark dots along the other side hem similarly.

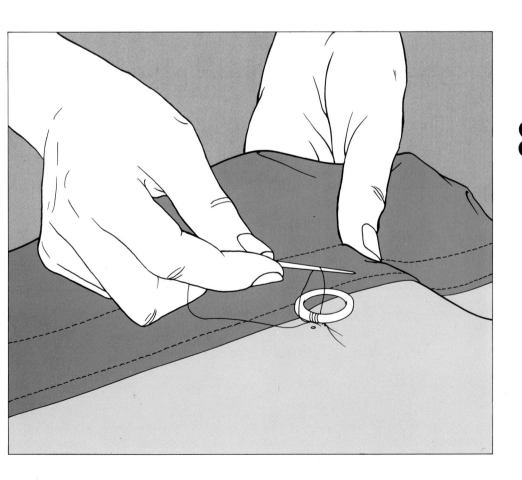

8 **Sewing on the rings.** Using doubled thread the color of the fabric, sew ½-inch bone or brass rings to the side hems and lining at each dot. Begin by tying a knot in the end of the thread, then push the tip of the needle through the dot to the front of the shade and back again to the lining side; pull the needle through until the knot catches.

Now place a ring on the dot and pass the needle through the ring, the lining and the face of the fabric with each stitch; this guarantees that both lining and shade will be drawn up together. Anchor each ring in place with a knot by passing the needle through the loop of thread two or three times *(left)*. Then draw the thread tight, cut it and go on to the next dot.

Because the rings in the bottom row will bear the most weight, reinforce each one with a few extra stitches. ▶

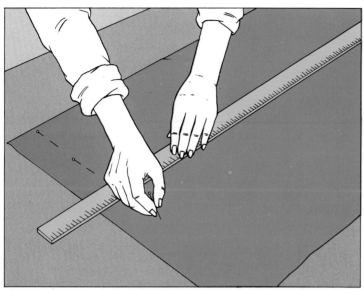

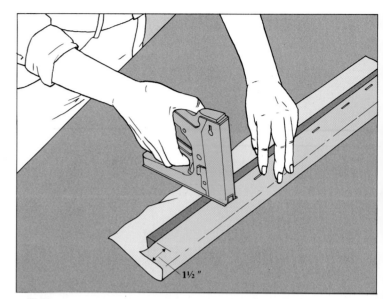

9 **Marking the finished length.** Turn the shade over to the front side. To determine where the top of the shade will fold over the mounting board — a crucial step if the shade is to fit the window precisely — measure the shade's finished length from the bottom with a yardstick or metal tape measure. Mark the finished length by inserting pins in several places across the top, including the tops of both side hems.

10 **Covering the mounting board.** For the mounting board, cut a pine 1-by-2 to a length ¼ inch shorter than the shade's finished width. Then cut a piece of fabric 3 inches longer than the mounting board and about 6 inches wide. For a shade mounted inside the window frame, lining fabric may be used as a cover. For an outside-mounted shade, use shade fabric to impart a uniform finished look. With its wide face down, center the board on the fabric so that 1½ inches of fabric extends beyond each end of the board. Wrap one long edge of the fabric up over the board so that the fabric covers almost the entire top face. Attach the fabric to the top face with a staple gun *(above)*, spacing the staples about 3 inches apart.

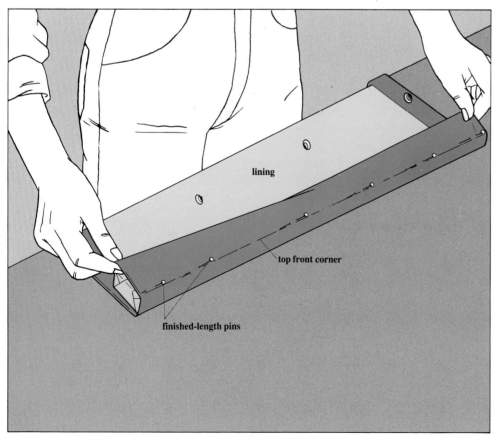

lining

top front corner

finished-length pins

12 **Positioning the shade on the board.** With the lining side up and the mounting board placed on the shade with its stapled wide face up, wrap the top of the shade around the board so that the finished-length pins rest along the top front corner of the board; this corner will face the room. With the pins resting on the top front corner, staple the shade to the top of the mounting board at 3-inch intervals. Remove the pins after the shade has been fastened to the board.

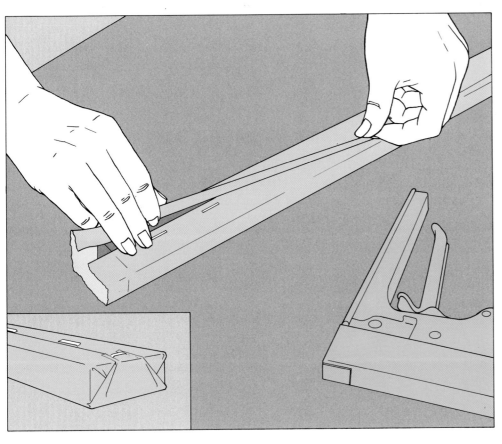

11 **Stapling the cover in place.** Wrap the free edge of the covering fabric around the exposed portion of the mounting board. Fold under the raw edge of the fabric, press it down against the top of the board so that it covers and extends beyond the first row of staples *(left),* and staple it in place. Use the fabric that extends beyond each end of the mounting board to gift wrap the board's ends *(inset).* Fold up the resulting triangle of fabric on each end onto the top of the board and secure it with a staple.

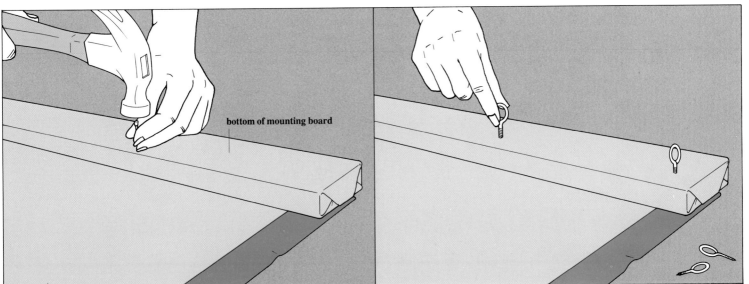

bottom of mounting board

13 **Inserting the screw eyes.** Lay the shade on the work surface, lining side up. Turn the mounting board so that its bottom faces up. Make a pencil mark on the bottom of the mounting board directly above each column of rings and about ½ inch from the front of the board. Make ½-inch-deep pilot holes at each pencil mark *(above, left)* with a brad or a small nail. Insert a screw eye ½ inch in diameter into each pilot hole *(above, right)* and screw it in place; with the last twist of your hand, turn the screw eye so that its opening faces the ends of the board. ▶

14 **Threading the pull cords.** For a right-hand pull, unwind lightweight nylon cord from a spool while threading it through the screw eye on the far left end of the board, then down through each ring in the column below the eye. Tie the cord to the bottom ring, cut it off below the knot and singe the end of the cord to prevent unraveling. Unwind enough additional cord to extend from the screw eye to the bottom of the shade, and cut the cord at that length.

Follow the same procedure to thread cords through the remaining columns of rings, passing each cord through one more screw eye before threading it down through the rings below it. Insert into the rod casing a ⅜-inch metal rod that has been cut ½ inch shorter than the finished width of the shade. There is no need to sew the ends of the casing closed.

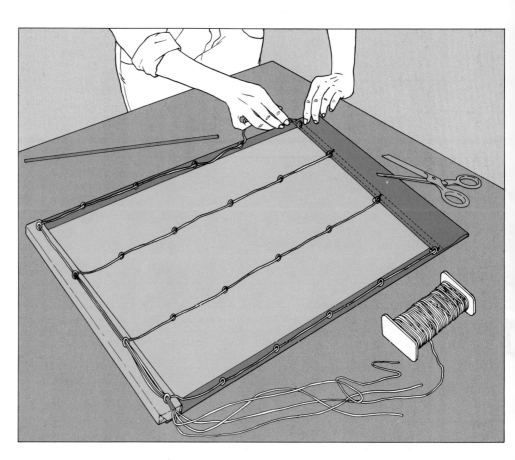

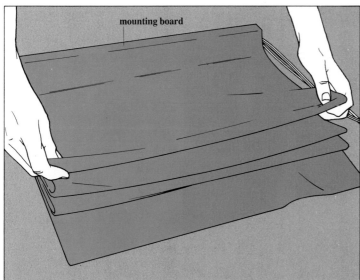

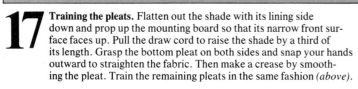

17 **Training the pleats.** Flatten out the shade with its lining side down and prop up the mounting board so that its narrow front surface faces up. Pull the draw cord to raise the shade by a third of its length. Grasp the bottom pleat on both sides and snap your hands outward to straighten the fabric. Then make a crease by smoothing the pleat. Train the remaining pleats in the same fashion (*above*).

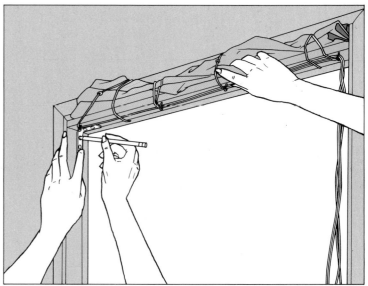

18 **Installing the shade.** With a helper holding the mounting board snug inside the window frame, position a 1½-inch angle iron flush against the vertical jamb and the bottom of the board. Mark the vertical leg's screw holes on the jamb with a pencil. Mark the position of a second angle iron at the other end of the board in the same manner. Take down the shade and angle irons. Hammer pilot holes at both marked positions, then screw the angle irons to the vertical jambs. Center the mounting board on the irons and mark screw-hole positions on the bottom of the board. Take down the shade again and hammer pilot holes at the marked positions. Reposition the board and secure it to the angle irons with screws.

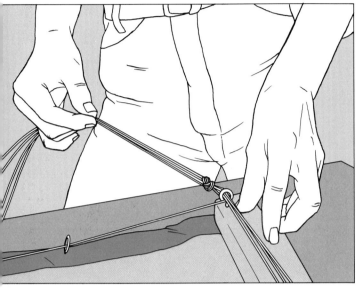

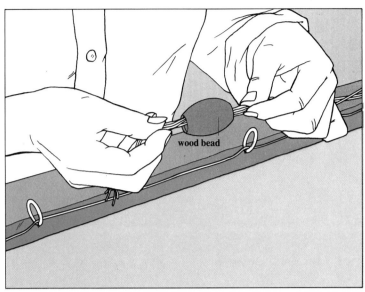

15 **Knotting the cords.** To achieve uniform tension on the rod, have a helper hold up the shade by the mounting board while you pull each cord taut. Then grip the cords in your hand just outside the screw eye and lay the shade back down. Tie a large knot in the cords where you gripped them. If you wish to braid the cords together for appearances' sake, start at the knot and work downward.

16 **Adding the pull.** Thread the cords through a heavy wood bead *(above)* or a weighted drapery pull, and slide the pull up the cords to a height that will afford a comfortable reach — generally one third to one half the distance from the top of the mount. Tie a bulky knot in the cords at that height to secure the pull. Cut off the excess cord about 1 inch below the knot and singe the ends to prevent unraveling, then slide the pull down tight to seat it on the knot.

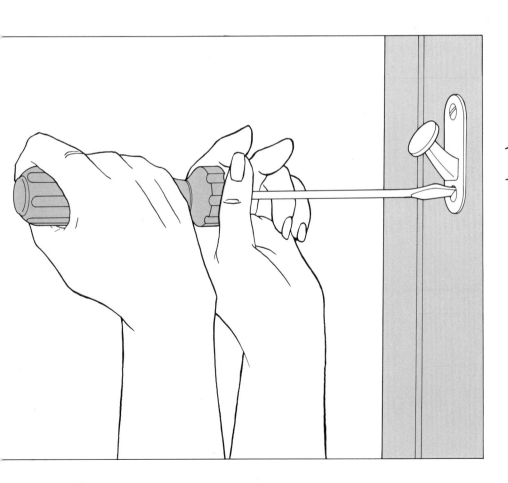

19 **Installing the awning cleat.** With the shade mounted and fully drawn up, find an inconspicuous location for the awning cleat; approximately one third of the way down the inside of the jamb is ideal. Holding the cleat in place with one hand, insert a pencil through each screw hole to mark the cleat's position on the jamb. Set the cleat aside. Using an awl or a small nail, tap pilot holes at the marks; reposition the cleat and screw it to the jamb.

When you raise the shade, wind the draw cord around the awning cleat. Keep the shade raised for two or three days to train in the pleats.

The balloon style: Lavish billows that control light

Even the most inexpensive fabric looks luxurious when done up into balloon shades, billowing in graceful curves across the bottom and shirred in compact folds at the top. To achieve the lavish effect shown here, the fabric must be used liberally, starting with triple the width and 20 inches more than the length of the area the shade is to cover. The fabric is gathered by means of four-cord shirring tape sewed to the back of the shade across the top. Drawing the cords bunches up the tape, and with it the fabric.

For a more tailored effect, multiply the area's width by one and one half, and add only 14 inches to the length. In either case, select a soft lightweight or medium-weight fabric that drapes easily, such as cretonne, gingham or, as here, chintz.

To create emphatic arcs, each balloon must be from 8 to 12 inches wide. Decide first how many balloons you would like, then determine how wide each will be by dividing the width of the area you plan to cover by the desired number of balloons. For example, if you have three balloons at a 32-inch window, each one will measure 10⅔ inches.

Regardless of the shade's dimensions, you will want the lining to be invisible from the room and the fabric from outdoors. To accomplish this, cut the lining 4 inches longer and 4 inches wider than the shade fabric. You can then center the fabric on the lining, cut off a 2-inch margin, and be certain that both layers are exactly the same size *(Step 1)*. Fabric and lining are then sewed together to form a pouch with a short opening at the top; when the pouch is turned right side out, the seam joining the fabric and lining is concealed.

A narrow casing at the bottom of the shade allows the insertion of a metal rod that serves as a weight to keep the shade even. Before the rod is inserted, it is wrapped in a sleeve with tabbed ends *(Step 9)*. The ends are sewed to the shade's bottom corners to prevent the gathered shade from slipping off the rod.

The balloon shade is mounted like the roman shade *(pages 105 and 110)* and, like the roman shade, is operated by nylon cords threaded through ring columns on the back and screw eyes anchored in the mounting board. Because each cord is tied to the last three rings in its column *(Step 10)*, the balloons retain their puffiness even when the shade is lowered.

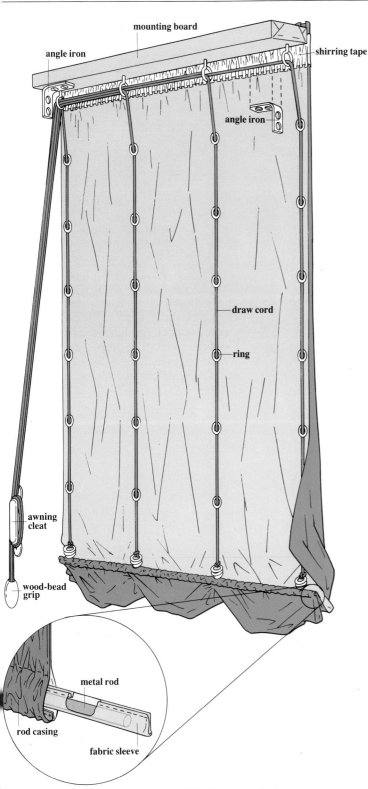

angle iron

mounting board

shirring tape

angle iron

draw cord

ring

awning cleat

wood-bead grip

metal rod

rod casing

fabric sleeve

Rear view of a shirred-top balloon shade. Like the roman shade *(page 105),* the balloon shade is operated by a system of cords and rings. However, tying each cord to the last three rings in each vertical column gives the bottom of the shade its balloon-like scallops. A cloth-encased metal rod *(inset)* fits a casing at the bottom of the shade to hold it steady. At the top, the shirred shade is stapled to a mounting board, and the cords are threaded through screw eyes on the underside of the board. Finally, the board is fastened to the window frame with angle irons; here, the right-hand angle iron is shown below its actual position to expose the screw eye at that end of the board.

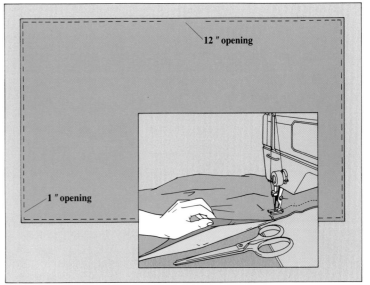

12 " opening

1 " opening

1 **Joining fabric and lining.** Cut and join widths of shade fabric and lining *(page 36, Step 2);* the lining should be 4 inches longer and wider than the shade fabric. Spread out the lining flat with the coated side — if any — facing up. Center the fabric, right side down, on the lining. Working out from the center, smooth the layers with your hands. Pin the layers together at 6-inch intervals along all four edges, marking a 12-inch opening at the center top and a 1-inch opening ¼ inch above one of the bottom corners *(above).* Using the shade fabric as a template, trim the excess lining with scissors. Sew fabric and lining together with a straight machine stitch ½ inch from each edge *(inset).* Lock-stitch at the edge of each opening to prevent the seam from unraveling. Remove the pins as you go.

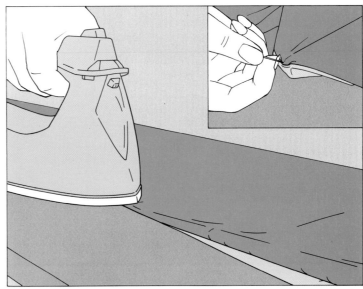

2 **Pressing the shade.** Reach into the 12-inch opening and pull out the bottom corners of the shade, one at a time, to turn the shade right side out. Use a straight pin to pick out the hard-to-reach little folds in each corner *(inset).* Spread the shade, lining side down, on an ironing board or padded work surface, and press the lining and fabric together *(above),* taking care that the fabric just overlaps the lining. Close the 12-inch opening by folding under and pressing the unsewed edges — first of the lining, then of the fabric — and using small overcast hand stitches to join them. Then machine-stitch a rod casing by sewing a straight seam across the back of the shade, 1¼ inches up from and parallel to the shade's bottom, beginning at the top of the 1-inch opening. ▶

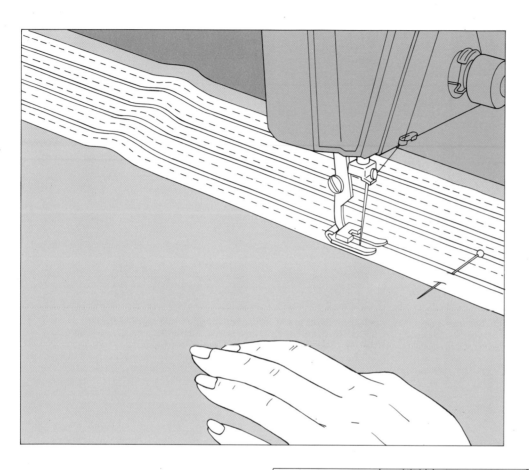

3 **Attaching the shirring tape.** Cut a length of four-cord shirring tape to fit across the lining and pin it ½ inch below the top edge; align the ends of the tape with the sides of the lining. Sew a straight-stitch line across the top of the tape ⅛ inch above the first shirring cord, removing the pins as you proceed. Then stitch lines centered between each pair of cords and ⅛ inch below the last shirring cord *(left)*.

5 **Aligning shade and mounting board.** Make a pencil mark ½ inch from each end of the narrow front face of the mounting board. Measure between the marks and divide the result by the number of balloons. Mark intervals of this width between the end marks. Next, measure for and mark the midpoint of the board's front narrow face; mark the midpoint of the top of the shade's lining with a pin. With the shade front facing up, align the marks *(right)*, remove the pin, and staple shade and board together there. Insert pins above the shirring tape directly over the top ring in each column so that each column's position is identifiable from the shade's front.

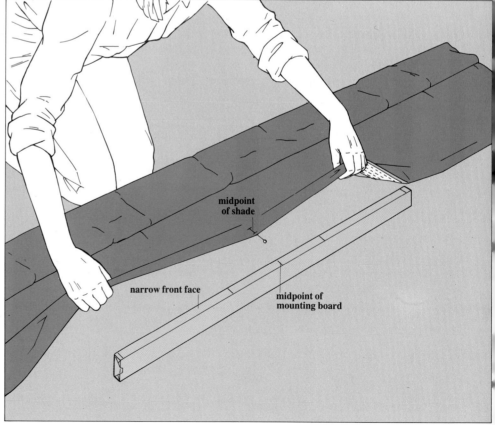

midpoint of shade

narrow front face

midpoint of mounting board

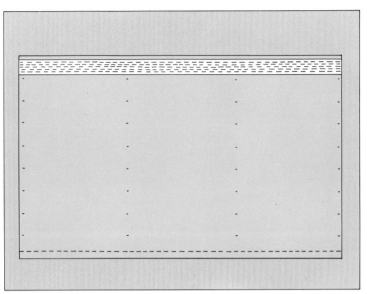

4 **Marking ring positions.** With a pencil, make a series of tick marks on the lining ½ inch from one side edge: Start 1¼ inches from the bottom of the lining, then put marks at 6-inch intervals, ending with a mark just below the shirring tape. Mark the other side edge similarly. Measure between the two bottom marks; divide that distance by the number of balloons you want. The result is the distance to use for spacing the ring columns. Beginning at a bottom mark, measure and mark positions for the bottom ring row. Align the short leg of a carpenter's square with the bottom of the shade. Working from a bottom mark toward the top, make marks at 6-inch intervals *(above, left)* until you have completed a symmetrical grid of evenly spaced rows and columns *(above, right)*.

Using the technique demonstrated on page 107, Step 8, sew a ⅜-inch brass or bone ring at each marked position. Then cover a 1-by-2 pine mounting board as shown on pages 108-109, Steps 10-11.

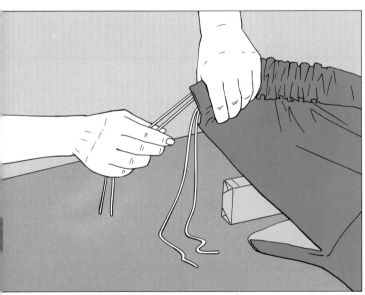

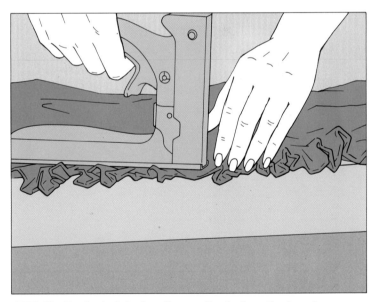

6 **Gathering the top.** At one end of the shade, pull the shirring cords two at a time, alternating top and bottom pairs and using short, firm tugs. Continue shirring one half of the shade until the pin above the ring column nearest the center of the shade aligns with the pencil mark nearest the midpoint of the mounting board.

7 **Stapling the shade in place.** Remove the pin above the ring column nearest the center of the shade. Separate the gathers and staple the top of the shade to the narrow front face of the board at the point where the pin and pencil mark aligned *(above)*. Continue gathering the shade along the cords, aligning the pins inserted in Step 5 with their corresponding pencil marks on the board and stapling the shade to the board at the points of alignment. Then, working from the midpoint toward the shirred end, part the gathers and staple the shade to the board at 1-inch intervals. Ruffle the gathers to conceal each staple within them. Pull the shirring cords one last time to align the end of the shade with the end of the board, and staple the ends together. ▶

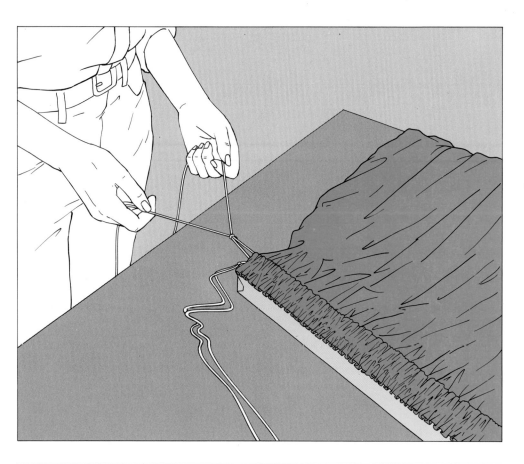

8 **Knotting the shirring cords.** Tie adjacent pairs of shirring cords together in a knot that lies flush against the end of the shirring tape. For a finished look, either cut off the cords below the knot or coil them up and secure them against the shade's inside edge with a safety pin. Repeat Steps 6 and 7 to gather the other half of the shade and attach it to the mounting board.

Insert a ½-inch screw eye into the bottom of the board directly in line with each ring column *(page 109, Step 13)*. For unusually wide shades — more than 36 inches — substitute small pulleys for the screw eyes.

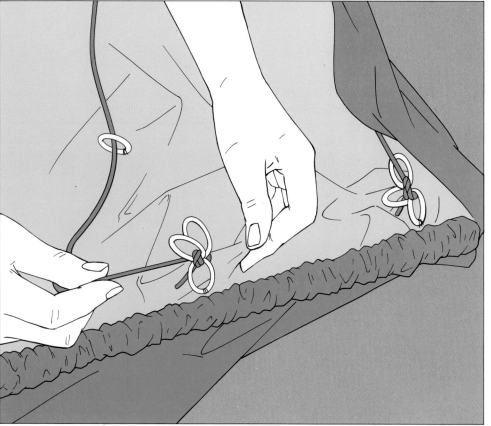

10 **Forming the balloons.** Thread lightweight nylon cord through the screw eyes and rings as shown on page 110, Step 14. However, instead of tying each cord to the bottom ring, tie it to the bottom three rings in its column *(left)*. This method hikes up the shade and forms the scalloped balloon shape at the bottom.

Cut off the excess cord below each knot and singe the cut ends with a match to keep them from unraveling.

If you plan to keep the shade in a fixed position, extra body can be added by stuffing each balloon with tissue paper.

9 **Encasing the rod.** Cut a strip of lining 3 inches wide and equal to the length of the rod plus 3 inches. At each end of the strip, fold inward 1 inch of the lining and crease it in place with an iron. Fold inward each long edge about ¾ inch; crease. Crease the strip lengthwise, long edges facing in. With your sewing machine, stitch together the long edges *(right)* and one of the open ends. Insert the rod into the sleeve, centering it so that a ½-inch tab of fabric extends beyond each end of the rod.

Insert the covered rod, closed end first, into the open end of the casing. Gather the shade along the rod so that the bottom rings align with their corresponding ring columns on the lining. Spread out the fullness evenly.

With the rod thus positioned, use overcast stitches to join the bottom corners of the shade to the ½-inch tabs at the rod ends. Then sew up the open end of the casing.

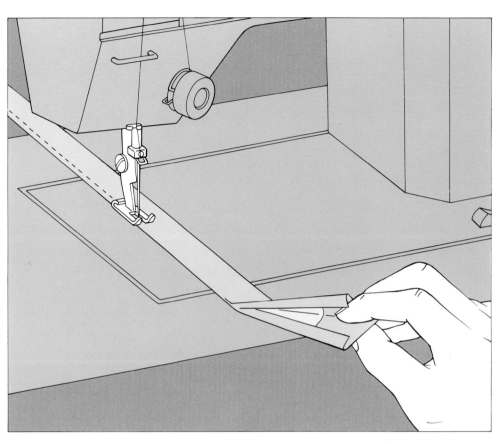

11 **Dressing the balloons.** Install the shade on angle irons *(page 110, Step 18)*. Adjust the cords until they exert even tension on the rod. Pull down the cords until the bottom of the shade aligns with the bottom of the window.

Tie the cords in a bulky knot just outside the screw eye. Then braid the cords if you wish, thread the loose ends through a heavy wood bead or weighted drapery pull, and knot them. Cut the ends below the knot and singe them to prevent unraveling. Slide the pull down so that it sits on the knot. Install an awning cleat as shown on page 111, Step 19.

Finally, raise the shade and pull the balloons out and down by hand *(right)* to adjust their billowing folds — a process known as dressing the balloons.

Sunlit patterns from dowels and layered fabric

Beguilingly simple in design and materials, the shades at left produce the effect of a multihued pattern with one solid-colored cloth and a handful of dowels. Paired here on corner windows, these shades filter sunlight through two, three, four and — at the hem outlining the inner arch — five layers of gauzy fabric. Like roman shades, they are raised with cords, but in this case the cords are threaded through dowels suspended across the shade.

For privacy, each shade is double-thick and extends from the top of the window casing to an inch above the floor, overlapping the window frame by an inch at each side. Here, the front layer of each shade is decorated with pieces — in the form of nested arches — cut from fabric panels almost the size of the shade. Other regular shapes — circles, triangles and the like — might embellish the shades instead.

The top and bottom rods are 1-inch wood dowels. Seven more dowels, from ½ to 1 inch in diameter, slip into unevenly spaced casings between the two layers of each shade; like the fabric decorations, these dowels can be sized and located as desired. Every dowel extends 1½ inches beyond the shade on both sides and has ⅛-inch holes at its ends to hold the cord.

To develop your own version, or to calculate proportions for using this design, begin with graph-paper scale drawings of your windows. Then make kraft-paper patterns for cutting the fabric accurately.

For the fabric, choose a sun-resistant sheer, such as a cotton or a cotton blend, of a width that will cover the window without piecing. To thread the shade, you will need mason's cord, a lightweight braided nylon cord. Each shade also calls for one cleat, two medium-sized screw eyes and two medium-sized L hooks; these, and the cord and dowels, are all available from hardware stores. Two decorative beads, for securing the cord ends, complete the shopping list.

The sewing consists of basic techniques, done with a flourish. All seams are topstitched, and all but the casing seams have double rows of stitches.

The instructions that follow are for the wider shade at left; its arches cover three-fourths of the shade's width and curve left. As you work on your shade, keep careful track of the right and wrong sides of panels, so that your pattern comes out facing the way you planned it.

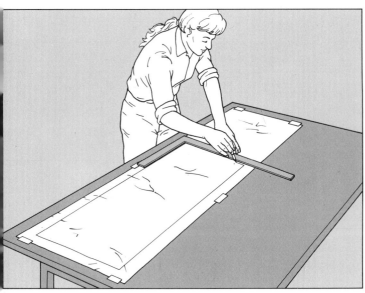

1 **Plotting patterns for the arch decorations.** For the larger arch, unroll a piece of kraft paper approximately the length of the shade onto a work surface. Tape down the paper. Using a dressmaker's square and a felt-tipped pen, draw a rectangle two thirds of the finished length of the shade, plus 3 inches for the bottom hem, and three fourths of the shade's finished width, plus 2 inches for the side hems.

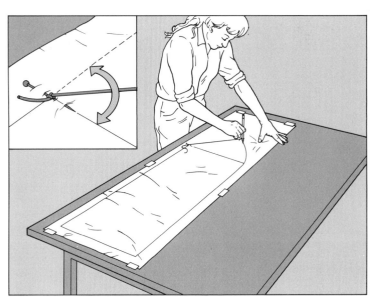

2 **Forming the top curve.** Tie a loop in one end of a piece of string and lay the string across the top line of the rectangle, with the end of the loop at one corner; where the string touches the other corner, tie a single knot. Pin this knot to the paper at the top left corner *(inset)*. Put the point of your pen into the loop, stretch the string taut across the top of the rectangle and place the penpoint on the top right corner. Keeping the pen vertical, draw an arc *(above)* from the top right-hand corner of the rectangle to the left-hand edge of the paper. Then extend the left-hand line of the rectangle until it meets the arc. To draw the smaller pattern, decrease the width of the rectangle by 3 inches and knot your string compass to match the new width. Cut out both paper patterns.

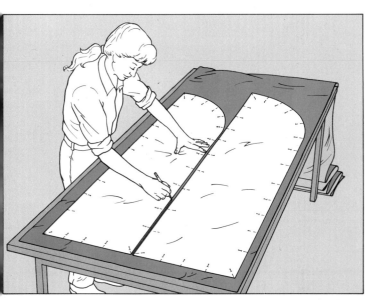

3 **Outlining the arch pieces onto the fabric.** Unfold one end of the fabric flat on the work surface and use the dressmaker's square to see if this end is square; trim it as necessary. Also cut off the selvages. Pin the patterns to the fabric and use a No. 3 pencil to outline the two arch pieces onto it. Remove the pins and the patterns, but do not do any cutting.

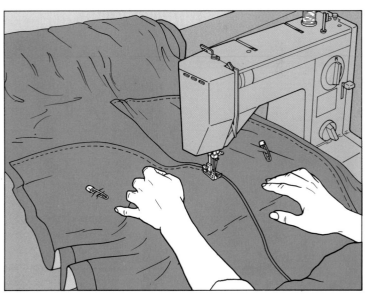

4 **Stay-stitching the curved edge of each arch.** Use a safety pin to mark the right, or finished, side of the fabric in each arch. Adjust your sewing machine for 12 stitches to the inch and sew all along the curve and down to the bottom on the right-hand side of each outlined arch, ½ inch inside the pencil line. This line of stitches, called stay stitching, will give the fabric added stability and help the curved edge hold its shape. Cut out the two arches exactly on the pencil lines. Cut the two rectangular pieces for the front and back panels of the shade, making each panel 3 inches wider than the shade's finished width and 6 inches longer than the finished length. Set both of these panels aside. ▶

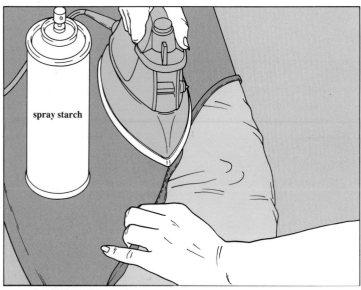

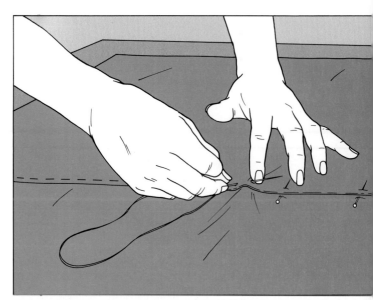

5 **Pressing hems on arch pieces.** Lay one arch piece right side down on an ironing board. Spray the curved edge generously with household starch. Creasing the fabric by hand exactly on the line of the stay stitching as you proceed, press a ½-inch hem from the top of the piece all along the curve and down that side of the arch. Press the other arch similarly.

6 **Basting a curved piece in place.** Lay one rectangular panel right side up on your work surface to serve as the front of the shade. Lay the larger arch piece over it, right side up (that is, with its pressed hem turned under). Align the two pieces along the bottom and the left side, and pin them together at regular intervals. Then baste by hand along the hemmed side, removing the pins as you go. To keep from disarranging the fabric as you baste, keep both hands on top of the fabric and use the needle to lift the work slightly for each stitch, as shown here. Baste ⅛ inch in from the turned edge, using two or three stitches to the inch.

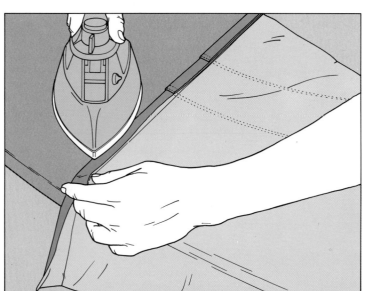

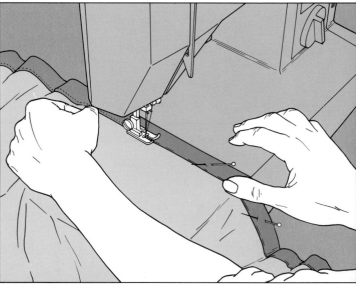

8 **Pressing side hems.** Lay the decorated panel right side down on the ironing board. Working along one long side of the panel and measuring with a hemming gauge, turn the fabric back 1½ inches and press it. Go back and unfold this hem, then press a second crease (*above*) midway between the first crease and the raw edge. Next, refold the fabric on the first crease, creating a double hem ¾ inch wide. Press the hem and pin it. Repeat for the other long side of the panel.

9 **Sewing the side hems.** On both side hems of the front panel, sew one row of 12-to-the-inch machine stitches, keeping the stitching as close to the inner edge of the hem as you can and removing the pins as you come to them. Then measure, press, pin and sew side hems on the back panel, which you set aside in Step 4.

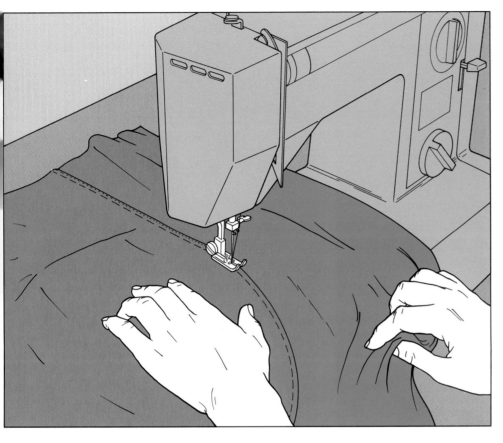

7 **Sewing the curved pieces in place.** Using 12 stitches to the inch, topstitch as shown along the hemmed side of the larger curved piece, keeping the stitches as close to the edge as you can. Take out the basting, then topstitch a second row of stitches ¼ inch inside the first.

Lay the front panel flat again and align the straight side and bottom edge of the smaller curved piece with the straight edges of the large curved piece and the panel behind it. Following the same techniques, baste and topstitch the smaller curved piece over the larger one.

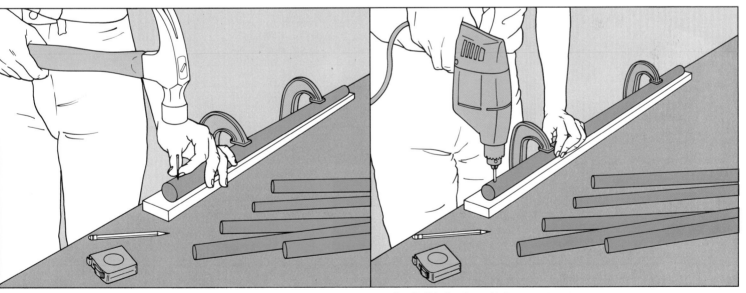

10 **Preparing the dowels.** Using a miter box and backsaw, or two C clamps and a crosscut saw, cut each wood dowel 3 inches longer than the finished width of the shade. Keeping a wood scrap under the work, clamp one dowel at a time to your work surface. Make a pencil mark ¾ inch from each end of the dowel. Dent each mark with a hammer and nail *(above)* to help keep the bit on the mark when you drill a ⅛-inch hole through the dowel *(above,*

right). Drill holes through all except the 1-inch dowel that will be the top rod. For the top rod, first drill a pair of ⅛-inch starter holes — only ⅛ inch deep — for the screw eyes. Next, loosen the clamps, turn the dowel a quarter turn and reclamp it. Mark and dent it again, then drill a ³⁄₁₆-inch hole through the dowel at each end, for the L hooks on which the shade will hang. Sand each dowel thoroughly with medium (100-grit) sandpaper. ▶

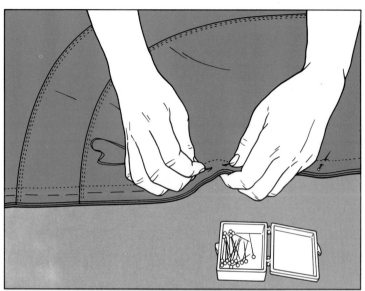

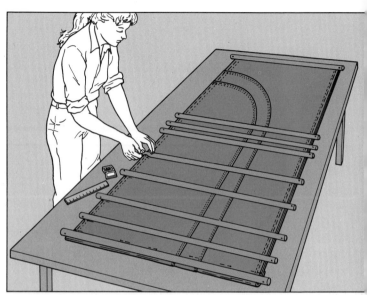

11 **Joining the two panels.** Lay the two panels flat, with their right sides out and all edges aligned. Pin them together, then baste along both long sides, ½ inch from the edge *(above)*. Remove the pins. With the shade face down on the ironing board, turn, press and pin 3-inch hems at the top and bottom.

12 **Marking locations for dowel casings.** Lay the shade face up on the work surface, put the top and bottom rods in place, and arrange the other dowels between them. Here, the three smallest dowels are nearest the top, 3½ inches apart; the next smallest is 12 inches lower; and the last three are at diminishing intervals — 10, 8, and 6 inches — with the largest at the bottom. Place a pin across the side hem below each dowel to mark that casing's lower seam. Remove all dowels. Place a second pin at each dowel location to mark the casing's upper seam: For ½-inch dowels, put the second pin ⅞ inch away; for ⅝-inch dowels, 1¹⁄₁₆ inches; for ¾-inch dowels, 1¼ inches; for a 1-inch dowel, 1¾ inches. Unpin the top and bottom hems.

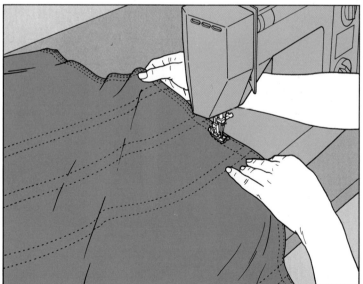

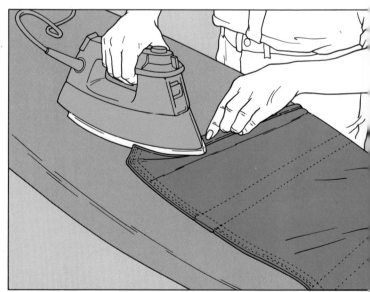

14 **Sewing the side seams.** Unfold the top and bottom hems and machine-stitch the panels together with short, paired seams at the side hems, running between the dowel casings and all the way to the shade's top and bottom raw edges. Finish all the outer seams along one side first, sewing next to the edge of the shade and taking care not to sew across any dowel casings. Then remove the basting and sew the inner seams ¼ inch in from the outer ones. Repeat for the other side hem. Begin and end each of these short seams with lock stitching *(page 21, bottom)*.

15 **Pressing and sewing the rod casings.** On the ironing board, lay the bottom of the shade face down and turn back the raw edges for the bottom rod casing. For 1-inch dowels, allow 1¾ inches for the casing and ⅜ inch for the double topstitching — a total of 2⅛ inches. Measure, turn and press the second crease for the hem *(above)* 2⅛ inches from the first, and pin the hem. Repeat for the top rod casing. To complete the sewing of the shade, sew each rod casing with two straight seams, ¼ inch apart.

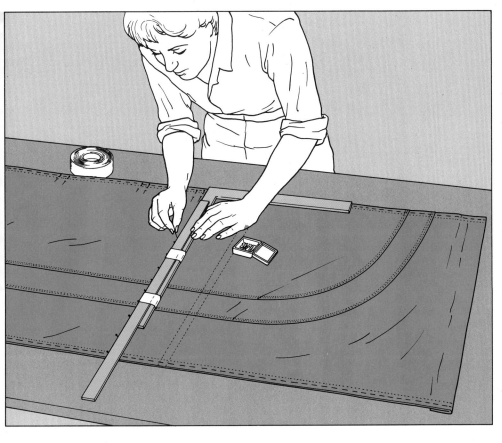

13 **Sewing the dowel casings.** If the longer arm of your dressmaker's square will not reach all the way across the shade, use duct tape to attach a yardstick, extending the arm. Then lay the short arm along the side hem and place the long arm across the shade at the top dowel-casing marker pin. Place a row of pins across the shade, as shown at left, exactly along the edge of the straightedge.

When you have set one row of pins, carry the shade carefully to the sewing machine. Sew one seam across the panel, sewing over the point where each pin enters the fabric but removing the pin as you get to it, rather than sewing across it. Repeat for each marker pin, until all the casing seams are sewed.

16 **Threading the cord through the dowels.** Lay the shade face down and slide all the dowels into their pockets. Rotate the top rod so that the starter holes for the screw eyes are at the back of the shade; screw the screw eyes into place. Cut a piece of mason's cord 3½ times as long as the shade. Put the ends together, and thread them through the screw eye on the side of the shade where you want the loop to hang, pushing them toward the center of the dowel. Leave a loop about half the length of the shade. Thread one end of the cord through the other screw eye, the dowels on that side, and the bottom rod. Tie a bead to the cord's end. Thread the other cord end down the other side of the shade in the same way.

17 **Hanging and training the shade.** Drill two ⅛-inch starter holes in the top frame of the window, 1½ inches from the top and as far apart as the holes in the top rod. Hand-screw two medium-sized L hooks into place *(inset)*. On the side of the frame where the loop will hang, mount the cleat *(page 111, Step 19)* a third of the way down. Hang the shade by fitting the holes in the rod onto the L hooks. Raise the shade by pulling the loop of cord, then secure the cord to the cleat. Where the fabric bunches up between dowels, push it through toward the window and arrange a stack of neat folds. Let the shade rest for a day; the next time you lower and raise it, the fabric will fall of its own accord into these same neat folds.

Installing fasteners for window treatments

Once you have determined and marked the locations for brackets or other supports used in a window treatment, installing them is a simple undertaking that requires only a few basic tools and the right fasteners.

You can handle most installations with a screwdriver and a variable-speed drill like the one at right, standard equipment in home workshops. You will need a set of twist bits of varying sizes to drill pilot holes for screws in wood and to drill holes for other kinds of fasteners *(opposite)* in plaster or wallboard.

If you are attaching hardware to brick or concrete, you will need a masonry bit of the appropriate size for the fastener; masonry bits have carbide-tipped edges that enable them to grind their way through concrete and brick that would stymie a twist bit.

The work is easiest when the hardware is being attached to a wooden window frame. You need only drill pilot holes for the screws, insert the screws through the holes in the hardware and drive them home. No. 8 wood screws are suitable for attaching most brackets to window frames; they require pilot holes drilled with a ⁵⁄₆₄-inch bit.

A screw length of 1 inch is usually sufficient. Curtain-rod manufacturers often supply screws; if you are uncertain what size the screws are and what size holes to drill, ask the supplier. Very small screws do not need pilot holes; they can be driven into dents started with an awl or nail.

Hardware on a wall or ceiling, rather than on a window frame, will be most secure if it is fastened by screws driven into wood studs or joists behind the wallboard. However, since the placement of window-treatment hardware is determined by other factors, you cannot be certain that a stud or joist will be available at just the right spot.

One sensible approach to wall or ceiling installations is to drill first with a bit of the right size for a wood-screw pilot hole. If, after penetrating the wallboard, you encounter increased resistance to the drill and find wood shavings on the bit, you have hit a stud or joist and can proceed to use a wood screw — 1½ inches long in most cases — for the job.

Heavier resistance to the drill, and brick or concrete drill dust, tells you

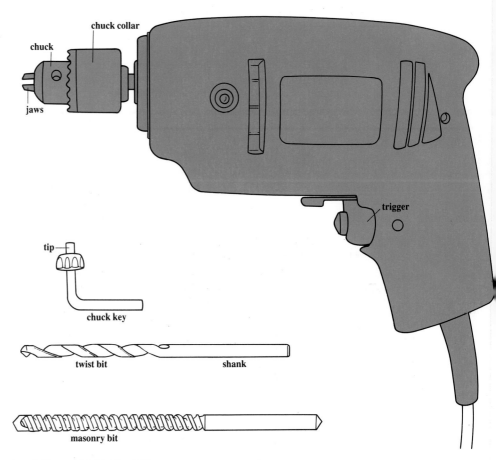

A variable-speed drill. The drill's speed — fast for a twist bit boring through wood, much slower for a masonry bit in concrete — varies with the pressure on the trigger. To insert a bit, turn the chuck collar to open the jaws, push the bit shank between the jaws and tighten the collar by hand until the jaws grip the shank. Then push the tip of the chuck key into one of the three holes in the chuck, and twist the key handle. To change bits, loosen the collar with the chuck key, then turn it by hand.

that you are dealing with masonry and therefore need to use an expansion shield or a plastic or lead anchor *(opposite)* to hold the screw.

If instead the drill breaks through the wallboard to a hollow or insulation-filled space behind, you should use some kind of hollow-wall fastener, such as a Molly® bolt or a toggle bolt *(opposite),* and you will need to drill a larger hole to fit whichever device you choose. Molly bolts have a distinct advantage over toggles: Their sheaths will remain in position so that the bolts can be reinserted if the fixture

is unscrewed in order to paint the room.

Metal studs requiring the use of self-tapping screws are usually found only in recently constructed office or apartment buildings. If your home does not have metal studs, stop drilling if you encounter very heavy resistance or metal shavings on the bit; you may have hit a pipe or electrical conduit.

When you are drilling overhead or at eye level, be sure to wear safety goggles to protect your eyes from drill dust. Always unplug the drill when it is not in use and before changing bits.

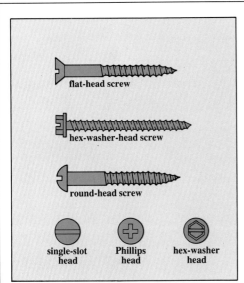

Wood screws. Flat-head screws fit flush into countersunk holes, like those in many angle irons; round-head screws are for holes without countersinks. Either type may have one slot or, for a Phillips ™ screwdriver, two crossed slots. Phillips heads are less likely to rip under turning pressure. Hex-washer-head screws fit a power screwdriver but can also be driven by a hand screwdriver. Screw-shaft diameter is denoted by gauge number; the higher the number the greater the diameter.

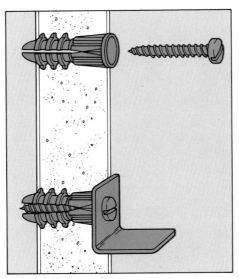

Anchor. The sides of an anchor press out to gain a tight grip in masonry, wallboard or plaster when a matching-sized wood screw or self-tapping screw *(shown)* is driven into it. Only very light loads should be anchored in wallboard this way; Molly bolts *(right)* and toggle bolts *(below, left)* are better for such hollow walls. In masonry, lead anchors carry heavier loads than plastic ones. Tap the anchor into a hole drilled to fit it snugly. Then insert the screw through the object to be hung, and drive it into the anchor.

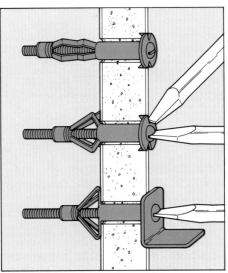

Molly bolt. The unbroken cylinder near the bolthead of this hollow-wall anchor should be as long as the wall is thick. Tap the Molly bolt into a hole drilled to its diameter. Wedge a screwdriver into one of the indentations in the flange to keep the sheath from turning as you tighten the bolt with another screwdriver. The sheath arms will splay out against the inside of the wall. Do not overtighten, or you may break the arms. Remove the bolt to put the load on it, then screw it back into position.

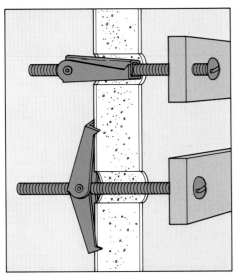

Toggle bolt. A toggle bolt must be long enough for its wings to spring open and grip the inside of a hollow wall. Drill a hole large enough for the folded wings to pass through, but do not push them in at this stage. Unscrew the wings from the bolt, slip the bolt through the object to be hung and replace the wings. Then push the bolt through the wall; when the wings pop open, the bolt will feel loose in the hole. Pull the device back so that the wings will bite into the inside of the wall as you tighten the bolt.

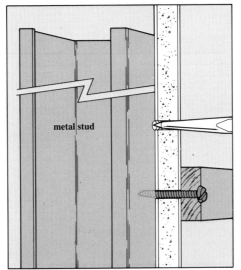

Self-tapping screw. This sort of screw is used to attach weights to metal studs. Drill a small hole in the wallboard to the face of the stud. Make a starter dent in the stud with a center punch and a hammer. Then use a twist bit to drill a pilot hole half the diameter of the screw through the thin metal. Insert the screw through the object you are hanging, and drive it into the stud; the screw should be long enough to reach about ½ inch beyond the face of the stud.

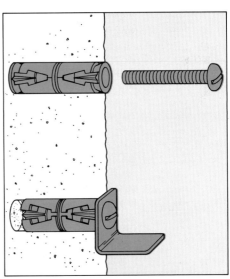

Expansion shield. This metal device with interior threads is used with a matching machine screw to hold a load on masonry or a thick plaster wall. Drill a hole that will hold the shield snugly, and tap the shield into it. Make sure the screw is long enough to extend through the hardware being installed and the shield. As you tighten the screw, wedges in the shield will be pulled toward the middle, pushing the cylinder sides hard against the masonry or plaster.

Acknowledgments

The index for this book was prepared by Louise Hedberg. The editors are particularly indebted to Jay Jafari, Creative Prints, Alexandria, Virginia, and Lowell Wade, ASID, Parr Excellence, Alexandria, Virginia. For their help in the preparation of this volume, the editors also wish to thank: Lynn R. Addison, Hyattsville, Maryland; Karen Armstrong, Pavilion Designs, Knightsbridge, London; Joel Baughman, Stylecraft Interiors, Kensington, Maryland; Deirdre Beard of Mrs. Monro Ltd., London; Joan Bell, Market Square Shop, Alexandria, Virginia; David A. Bennett, Alexandria, Virginia; Enzo Bertazzo, Milan; Horst Boehlendorf, Custom Design Studios Inc., Arlington, Virginia; Stasia Brokaw, Philadelphia College of Textiles and Science, Philadelphia, Pennsylvania; Mr. and Mrs. Jeremy E. Brown, Potomac, Maryland; Carolyn's Curtains & Cascades, Fredericksburg, Virginia; Mary Edwards, Mileham & King Showroom, Rockville, Maryland; Carol Fram, Westminster, Maryland; Isidoro Genovese, Rome; Walter Grazzani, Studio Azzurro, Milan; Gary Gregg, ASID, Silver Spring, Maryland; Tom Gusdorff, Fabricare Draperies, Kensington, Maryland; Marilyn Henderson, ASID, Interiors Ltd. of McLean, Bethesda and Annapolis, Bethesda, Maryland; William Jawish, John Ligon, Inc., Bethesda, Maryland; Pat Jellison, Dannemann Fabrics, Alexandria, Virginia; Bette Katz, Home Fashion Products Association, Jamesburg, New Jersey; Loretta Kayser, Reston, Virginia; Jack Koontz, Woodward & Lothrop, Washington, D.C.; Aku Merali, Market Place Interiors, Alexandria, Virginia; Linda Miller, Dick Waters Shade Shop, Arlington, Virginia; Janet Modie, Blind Alley Limited, London; Mary Ruth Morgan, John Ligon, Inc., Bethesda, Maryland; P. A. O'Gulian, Woodward & Lothrop, Washington, D.C.; Lawrence Paolantonio, Woodward & Lothrop, Chevy Chase, Maryland; Cathy Pollari, Textiles Library, North Carolina State University, Raleigh, North Carolina; Gail Raiman, American Textile Manufacturers Institute, Washington, D.C.; Georgia Rodeffer, Burlington Industries, Greensboro, North Carolina; Susanne Rudden, ASID, Interior Design Concepts, Alexandria, Virginia; Frederick W. Sachs Jr., W. A. Smoot & Co., Inc., Alexandria, Virginia; Skip Saunders, Outer Banks Deck Builders, Alexandria, Virginia; Cecile C. Stiner, Dannemann Fabrics, Alexandria, Virginia; Dorothy Stringer, Falls Church, Virginia; Mary Ruth Thorpe, John Ligon, Inc., Bethesda, Maryland; Cindy Thrall, Dick Waters Shade Shop, Arlington, Virginia; Frederick L. Wall, Arlington, Virginia; Marcia Wallace, Energy Saver Shades Shop, Springfield, Virginia; Grace Wells, The Valentine Museum, Richmond, Virginia; Joy Wulke, New Haven, Connecticut; Nelson Wurz, Nelson Beck of Washington, Inc., Washington, D.C.

Picture Credits

The sources for the photographs in this book are listed below, followed by the sources for the illustrations. Credits from left to right on a single page or a two-page spread are separated by semicolons; credits from top to bottom are separated by dashes.

Photographs: **Cover:** James Mortimer, photographer, from *The World of Interiors,* London. **2, 3:** Fran Brennan, photographer, courtesy *Houston Home & Garden Magazine* / design by Robert E. Kinnaman and Brian A. Ramaekers. **4, 5:** Harry Hartman, photographer, from Bruce Coleman, Inc., New York; Neil Lorimer, photographer, from Elizabeth Whiting Associates, London. **6, 7:** Emmett Bright, photographer / design by Stefano Mantovani, Rome. **8:** Dan Cunningham, photographer / design by Gary Gregg, ASID, Silver Spring, Maryland. **9:** James Mortimer, photographer, from *The World of Interiors,* London / design by Jaime Parlade, Malaga, Spain. **15:** Library of Congress, from George Smith, *Smith's Cabinet-Maker's and Upholsterer's Guide,* 1826. **16:** Dan Cunningham, photographer. **32:** © Norman McGrath, photographer / Peter Gisolfi, architect. **35:** Dan Cunningham, photographer / design by Marilyn Henderson, ASID, Interiors Ltd. of McLean, Bethesda and Annapolis, Bethesda, Maryland. **40:** Dan Cunningham, photographer / location, courtesy Mr. and Mrs. Matthew Simchak. **44:** James Mortimer, photographer, from *The World of Interiors,* London. **48:** Dan Cunningham, photographer / location, courtesy Mr. and Mrs. Charles N. Farmer / design by Lawrence Paolantonio, Interior Design Studio, Woodward & Lothrop, Chevy Chase, Maryland. **56:** Dan Cunningham, photographer / location, courtesy Mr. and Mrs. Marvin J. Perry / design by Isabelle Karekin, Marvin J. Perry & Associates, Kensington, Maryland. **61:** © Robert Grant Photography / design by Motif Designs, New Rochelle, New York. **62:** Dan Cunningham, photographer / location, courtesy Mrs. Evelyn Boyer / design by Marilyn Henderson, ASID, Interiors Ltd. of McLean, Bethesda and Annapolis, Bethesda, Maryland. **66:** Dan Cunningham, photographer / location, courtesy Williams-Whittle Associates, Inc., Alexandria, Virginia. **72, 79:** Dan Cunningham, photographer. **87:** Tom Leighton, photographer, from Syndication International, Ltd., London / design by Karen Armstrong, Pavilion Designs, Knightsbridge, London. **91:** James Oesch, photographer / location, courtesy Mr. and Mrs. Thomas Fricke / design by Lancllc K. Kyle, Betty Harrison Interiors, Falls Church, Virginia. **102:** Dan Cunningham, photographer / shade, courtesy John Ligon, Inc., Bethesda, Maryland / rocking chair, courtesy The Sow's Ear Antiques, Alexandria, Virginia. **104:** © 1983 William G. Cady, photographer / design by Ellen Carroll, Great Falls, Virginia. **112:** Dan Cunningham, photographer / location, courtesy Mr. and Mrs. James L. Peeler. **118:** © 1979 Robert Perron, photographer / design by Joy Wulke, New Haven, Connecticut.

Illustrations: **18, 19:** Sketches by David Baker, inked by Frederic F. Bigio from B-C Graphics. **20-23:** Sketches by Jack Arthur, inked by Walter Hilmers Jr. from HJ Commercial Art. **25-31:** Sketches by Fred Holz, inked by Frederic F. Bigio from B-C Graphics. **33, 34:** Sketches by Jack Arthur, inked by Arezou K. Hennessy. **36-39:** Sketches by Jack Arthur, inked by John Massey. **41-43:** Sketches by Joan McGurren, inked by Walter Hilmers Jr. from HJ Commercial Art. **45-47:** Sketches by Joan McGurren, inked by John Massey. **49-55:** Sketches by Roger Essley, inked by Frederic F. Bigio from B-C Graphics. **57-61:** Sketches by Fred Holz, inked by Arezou K. Hennessy. **63-65:** Sketches by William J. Hennessy Jr., inked by Walter Hilmers Jr. from HJ Commercial Art. **67-71:** Sketches by George Bell, inked by Frederic F. Bigio from B-C Graphics. **73-76:** Sketches by Jack Arthur, inked by Adisai Hemintranont from Sai Graphis. **77, 78:** Sketches by Jack Arthur, inked by Arezou K. Hennessy. **80-86:** Sketches by Joan McGurren, inked by Frederic F. Bigio from B-C Graphics. **88, 89:** Sketches by Jack Arthur, inked by Adisai Hemintranont from Sai Graphis. **90-97:** Sketches by Roger Essley, inked by Frederic F. Bigio from B-C Graphics. **99-101:** Sketches by Roger Essley, inked by Adisai Hemintranont from Sai Graphis. **102, 103:** Sketches by Jack Arthur, inked by Frederic F. Bigio from B-C Graphics. **105-111:** Sketches by Greg DeSantis, inked by John Massey. **113-117:** Sketches by Greg DeSantis, inked by Arezou K. Hennessy. **119-123:** Sketches by William J. Hennessy Jr., inked by Walter Hilmers Jr. from HJ Commercial Art. **124:** Sketches by Roger Essley, inked by Adisai Hemintranont from Sai Graphis. **125:** Sketches by Fred Holz, inked by Walter Hilmers Jr. from HJ Commercial Art.

Index/Glossary

A

Acetate, *chart* 17
Acrylic, 16, *chart* 17
Anchors, 124, 125
Angle irons, 62, 64, 88, 98, 100
Apron-length curtains, 25, 27, 32
Awning cleat, 104, 105, 111, 117

B

Backstitch: *to secure the end of a straight machine seam by stitching in reverse for ½ inch;* 34, 42, 53, 54
Balloon shades, 112-117; fabric for, 112; ring-and-cord system, 112, 113, 115, 116
Basic curtain construction, 32-34
Baste: *to sew pieces of fabric together temporarily, usually with long straight stitches;* 46, 47, 51, 120, 122
Batting, 90, 91, 92, 94
Bias: *a direction diagonal to the grains of the threads in a fabric;* 79, 82
Bias tape, 87, 88, 89
Blind-hem stitch, 20, 22, 23; by hand, 22; by machine, 23
Blinds, 98; venetian, 98, 101; vertical, 98, 100
Bobbin, 20, 21; screw, 20, 21
Bow-tied curtains, 61
Box pleats, 78
Brackets: for curtain rods, 24, 27; for shades, 98, 99, 100, 101
"Breaking" heading, 72, 76
Buckram, for reinforcement, 58, 87, 88
Button, covering with fabric, 65

C

Café curtains: basic, 32-34; calculating amount of material, 32, 33; fabric for, 32; measuring for, 26; outside-mounted, 27; rods for, 24, 26; scalloped, 40-43
Carrier slides, on traverse rods, 28, 30, 76; removing or adding extra, 28
Cartridge pleats, 78
Cascades (swags and jabots), 66-71
Casement windows, 24, 26
Casing: *a channel sewed at the top and / or bottom of a curtain to hold a rod; also called a rod pocket;* 24, 27, 49; for dowels, 122-123; measuring for, 36, 37; on roman shades, 104, 105, 107, 110; sewing, 34, 39, 47, 54
Ceiling: attaching hardware to, 124; track, for traverse rod, 31
Clip: *in sewing, to make a short cut into the seam allowance or the selvage to help fabric lie flat;* 20, 36, 38, 43, 63
Concrete, attaching hardware to, 124
Cornice, building and upholstering, 90-97; fabric for, 90; size of, 90
Cotton and cotton blends, 16, *chart* 17
Curtain rods, 24, 26-31; inside-mounted, 24, 25; lined sleeve for, 48-49, 54, 55; measuring for, 24, 25; mounting, 24; return, 24; sash-mounted, 24, 25, 26; stapling fabric to, 56, 60; swinging, 24, 27, 44; tension, 26, 32; traverse, 28-31; wall-mounted, 25
Curtains: apron-length, 25, 27, 32; bow-tied, 61; box-pleat, 78; café, 32-34; cartridge-pleat, 78; constructing basic, 32-34; floor-length, 25; hardware, 26-31; lined rod-casing, 35-39; measurements, 24-25; movable, 24; outside-mounted café, 27; pinch-pleat, 72-76; pouf, 48-55; ruffled, 44-47; scalloped café, 40-43; sheer pinch-pleat, 72, 77; stationary, 24; swags and

jabots (cascades), 66-71; tab, 27, 56-60; tent-flap, 24, 62-65; as undertreatments, 24, 77
Cutting fabric: patterned, 18, 19; unpatterned, 18

D

Dowels, 121. *See also* Gauze-and-dowel shade
Draperies, 14; pinch-pleat, 72-76
Drapery hook, 57, 60, 76
Dressmaker's square, extending, 123
Dual-duty thread, 20
Dry cleaning, 16

E

Expansion shield, 124, 125

F

Fabric: characteristics, 16, *chart* 17; compatibility with thread, 20; cutting and squaring, 18-19; draping properties of, 16; dye lot, 16; effect of steam on, 32; fiber content, 16; finishes, 16, 18, 102; measuring, 24-25; weave, 16; weights of, and thread and needle sizes, 20
Fabric-covered roller shade, 102-103; adhesive backing, 102; fabric for, 102; hardware, 102
Fasteners, 24, 124-125
Feed dog, 20, 21
Fiberglass. *See* Glass
Fibers: natural, 16, *chart* 17; synthetic, 16, *chart* 17
Finial: *a decorative endpiece for a curtain rod; may be made of brass or wood and shaped like a knob, a pineapple, an arrow, foliage or the like;* 27, 56, 60
Flame-resistant fabric, *chart* 17
Flax (linen), *chart* 17
Floor-length curtains, 25, 27; pinch-pleat, 72-77; pouf, 48-55; tab, 56-60
Floors, uneven, adjusting measurements for, 25
Fusible web, 102

G

Gauze-and-dowel shade, 118-123; fabric for, 118
Glass (fiber), *chart* 17
Grain: *the direction of threads in woven fabrics. The warp forms the lengthwise grain from one cut end of the fabric to the other; the weft forms the crosswise grain from selvage to selvage. Bias is the diagonal direction across the fabric;* 44, 67, 79, 82, 87, 104

H

Hand sewing, 20, 22
Hardware, attaching: for curtains, 14, 26-31; with fasteners, 124-125; to masonry walls, 124, 125; for shades, 98-101; to walls, 124; to wood, 124, 125
Heading: *in sewing, the top of the curtain; the top hem. Often stiffened with buckram and pleated;* "breaking," 72, 76; of buckram, 87; measuring for, 26, 27, 32, 33; ruffle-like, 44; sewing, 34, 54; and tabs, 56
Headrail, 98, 100, 101
Hemming gauge, 33, 105
Hems: machine-sewed, 23; pressing, 32; stitching by hand, 22; weighting, 32, 34, 36, 88
Holdback: *a decorative metal arm that holds a curtain or drapery to one side of the window;* 44, 79
Hollow-wall fasteners, 124, 125

I

Inside-mounted curtains, 26
Insulating linings, 35

Interfacing, 79, 80, 82, 84, 85; fusing, 80
Interlining, 35, 48-51, 52

J

Jabots, 24, 66-71
Joists, locating behind walls, 124

L

Lace, 32, 33, 34
Leading edge, 37, 65
Lined curtains: bow-tied, 61; pinch-pleat, 72-76; pouf, 48-55; rod-casing, 35-39; swags and jabots (cascades), 66-71; tab, 56-60; tent-flap, 62-65
Lined sleeve, for curtain rod, 48-49, 54, 55
Linen, *chart* 17
Lock-stitch: *to anchor the end of a straight seam by making three or four stitches in place;* 21
Loop turner, 61
Louvers, 98

M

Masonry: attaching hardware to, 124, 125; bit, 124
Mason's cord, 118, 123
Matching pattern repeats, 18, 19
Measuring: for curtain rods, 24; for fabric, 24-25; windows, 25
Meeting rail, 50
Mildew, 16, *chart* 17
Miter box and backsaw, 103, 121
Modacrylic, *chart* 17
Molly® bolt, 124, 125
Moths, 16, *chart* 17
Mounting boards, 24, 25, 63, 67, 87, 100, 105, 113, 114; covering, 108-109; curving, 88
Movable curtains, 24; traverse rods for, 28-31
Muslin, 104

N

Natural fibers, 16, *chart* 17; thread for, 20
Needles, sizes of, 20, 32
Nylon, *chart* 17

O

Opaque fabrics, 32, 40; hem weights for, 34
Outside-mounted curtains, 27
Overcast (zigzag) stitch, 20, 22; by hand, 22

P

Panel: *in sewing, one curtain of a pair, or two or more widths of fabric sewed together;* 24, 32, 33; cutting and squaring, 18, 19; joining widths, 35, 36
Patterned fabric: calculating amount, 18, 24; matching designs, 18, 19; squaring and cutting, 18, 19
Pattern repeat: *the space occupied by each complete unit of a design motif, from the top of one motif to the top of the next;* 18, 19, 24, 32, 36
Pilot holes, 124, 125
Pinch-pleat curtains, 72-76; hanging, 72, 76; sheer, 72, 77
Pinch-pleat valance, 87-89
Plaster wall, fasteners, 125
Pleated shades, 98; mounting, 101
Pleater tape, 75
Pleats: box, 78; cartridge, 78; four-fold pinch, 77; plotting, 73; three-fold pinch, 72, 74, 88; training, 72, 76, 110
Polyester, *chart* 17; thread, 20
Pouf curtains, 48-55; fabric for, 48
Power drill, 124
Presser foot, 20, 21

R

Rayon, *chart* 17
Repeats, pattern. *See* Pattern repeat
Return: *the distance from the front of the rod to the wall, applicable to rods that are positioned forward from the wall; the extra section of rod and width of curtain fabric used to enclose this distance;* 24, 27, 59, 60, 88
Ribbon ties, 61
Ring hooks, 56, 57, 59, 60
Rings: on balloon shades, 112, 113, 115, 116; curtains hung from, 26, 27, 40, 42; for roman shades, 104, 106-107, 110-111; on shade tape, 104; for tiebacks, 79, 81
Rod casing. *See* Casing
Rod-casing curtains: basic café, 32-34; calculating amount of fabric, 36; fabric for, 35; lined, 35-39
Roller (shade): adjusting spring, 103; cutting, 103
Roller shades, 98, 99; fabric-covered, 102-103; mechanism, 99
Roman shades, 98, 100, 104-111; fabric for, 104; mounting, 100, 110-111; pleat width, 104; ring-and-cord system, 105, 106-107, 110-111
Ruffle, 44, 45-47
Ruffled curtains, 44-47; crane for, 24, 27, 44; fabric for, 44; tieback, 79, 84-85

S

Sash rods, 24, 25, 26; for scalloped curtains, 40-43
Scalloped curtains, 40-43; estimating amount of material, 40; fabric for, 40
Scallops, planning pattern for, 40, 41
Screws, 24, 124, 125; self-tapping, 124, 125; wood, 124, 125
Seam allowance: *the extra width of fabric, usually ½ inch, that extends outside a seam line.*
Seam ripper, 52
Seams: and length of stitch, 20; overcasting raw edges, 22; sewing, 20-22; thread type and, 20
Self-tapping screws, 124, 125
Selvage: *the lengthwise finished edges of woven fabric;* 18, 19; clipping, 20, 36, 37, 38

Sewing machine, 20; adjusting thread tensions, 20, 21; threading, 20; upper and lower threads, 20, 21
Sewing techniques, 20-23; basic stitches, 20, 21, 22, 23
Shades: balloon, 112-117; cutting roller, 103; fabric-covered roller, 102-103; gauze-and-dowel, 118-123; hardware, 98-101; installation, 98, 99-101; material for, 98; ordering custom-made, 98; pleated, 98, 101; ready-made, 98; reverse-rolled, 99; roller, 98, 99; roman, 98, 100, 104-111
Shade tape, 104
Sheer curtains, pleated, 72, 77
Sheer fabrics, 32, 34, 40, 77, 118; thread for, 20
Shirring tape, 48, 49, 52-53, 54, 112, 114, 115, 116
Silk, *chart* 17
Sill-length curtains, 26, 32
Squaring fabric, 18-19
Stackback, 24, 25, 76
Stationary curtains, 24
Stay stitch: *a line of machine stitching used as a reinforcement for a curve, or as a guide for folding an edge;* 119, 120
Stitches: blind-hem, 20, 22, 23; length of, 20; locking, 21; overcast, 20, 22; straight, 20, 21
Stretch curtains, 40-43
Stud, metal, fasteners for, 124, 125
Swags and jabots (cascades), 24, 66-71; fabric for, 66
Swinging-crane rod, 24, 27, 44
Synthetic: fabric, thread for, 20; fibers, 16, *chart* 17

T

Tab curtains, 56-60; fabric for, 56; hardware, 27
Tension rods, 26, 32
Tensions, adjusting on sewing machine, 20, 21
Tenterhooks, 56, 57, 60
Tent-flap curtains, 24, 62-65
Thimble, china vs. metal, 72, 75
Thread: dual-duty, 20; thickness of, 20; for topstitching, 20; types of, 20
Thread tensioner, 20, 21
Throat plate, 20, 21

Tiebacks, threaded, 56, 59-60
Tiebacks (fabric), 79-86; contoured, 80-81; reinforced with interfacing, 80; rings for, 81; ruffled, 84-85; and support, 86; welted, 82-83
Toggle bolt, 124, 125
Topstitch: *to sew a visible line of stitches, usually parallel to a seam. It is used for decoration or to stiffen an edge;* 20, 118, 121, 122
Traverse rods, 24, 28-31; ceiling, 31; double, 28; mounting, 29-31; for pinch-pleat draperies, 72-76, 77; removing or adding extra carrier slides, 28; reversing cord, 28
Trim, attaching, 35, 36-37

U

Undertreatments, 24, 77

V

Vacuuming curtains and shades, 16
Valance, 87-89; fabric for, 87; height of, 87
Variable-speed drill, 124; twist bits, 124
Venetian blinds, 98, 101
Vertical blinds, 98, 100

W

Wall: attaching hardware to, 124; hollow-, fasteners for, 124, 125
Weave, fabric, 16
Weights, hem, 32, 34, 36
Welting, 79, 82-83
Width: *in sewing, often a single width of fabric of the required length for a curtain;* 33, 35, 36, 87, 104, 113
Window: frame, attaching hardware to, 124; hardware, 26-31, 98-101; measuring, 25; recess, for shades, 98
Window treatments: cleaning, 16; designs, 14-15; origins, 14. *See also* Blinds; Curtains; Shades
Wood, attaching hardware to, 124
Wool, *chart* 17

Z

Zigzag (overcast) stitch, 20, 22